Comparative Studies of How People Think

MICHAEL COLE AND BARBARA MEANS

Comparative Studies of How People Think

AN INTRODUCTION

Harvard University Press
Cambridge, Massachusetts, and London, England
1981

Library of Congress Cataloging in Publication Data

Cole, Michael, 1938-
    Comparative studies of how people think.

    Bibliography: p.
    Includes index.
    1. Psychological research – Cross-cultural studies.
2. Thought and thinking – Cross cultural studies.
I. Means, Barbara, 1949- joint author. II. Title.
BF76.5.C63   153'.072   80-23825
ISBN 0-674-15260-3

To our teachers

W. K. Estes and W. D. Rohwer, Jr.

Preface

The preparation of this book was made possible through the good offices of the Social Science Research Council, whose Committee on Cognitive Research sponsored our work. In the mid-1970s a series of workshops sponsored by the committee explored the severe interpretive problems posed by research on human beings that is comparative in nature. The committee's concern arose from a mixture of issues that are in some respects "applied psychology," and in other respects issues that speak to the heart of psychology as a basic science. On the applied side the committee was very concerned with the application of experimental methods to diverse populations for the purposes of drawing general conclusions about underlying cognitive capacities; all too often such conclusions seemed motivated more by political persuasion than by the logic of inference from experimentally obtained data. Only a deeper understanding of the nature of experimentation as a means of exploring (and perhaps defining) intellect can resolve the interpretive ambiguities that plague this kind of research. Hence the committee's insistence that fundamental problems of psychology as a science must be worked out to put such research on a sound footing.

This book is our own production, based upon discussions in workshops, private conversations, and several years of teaching and reviewing for journals. Its strengths are derived from all that we have learned from our colleagues over the years. Its weaknesses are a mixture of our personal shortcomings and the weaknesses of our science, weaknesses that this work seeks to reduce.

Contents

Figures

Tables

Comparative Studies of How People Think

1.

Old Interests
and New Demands

When a graduate student in psychology is asked at his doctoral orals: "What research would you like to do next?" the routine answer is: "I think it (the procedure of the dissertation) should be tried *with children*" or "*cross-culturally.*" Or it might be tried with schizophrenics or with working-class respondents or with *Planaria.*

— Roger Brown, *Transcultural Studies in Cognition*

On the face of it, launching into comparative research can look disarmingly simple to the student who has never tried it: the task, materials, and procedures he has developed in his experiments with adults can just be given to a new type of subject — whether preschoolers, dyslexics, or Guatemalan farmers. This may *seem* the easiest way to turn out new research fast. The student may hope to save himself the painstaking effort required to develop a new theoretical idea along with the appropriate tasks, procedures, and materials to test it. But in reality, comparative research is never so simple, and the purpose of this book is to explain why Roger Brown's prototypical graduate student can't just "try it" with children, schizophrenics, or squirrels.

A study of the intellectual activity of any of the special types of subjects just mentioned would fall into the class of research we are calling comparative. Comparative cognitive research may involve contrasting American mothers with Indonesian mothers, young people with older people, learning-disabled students with average students, or women with men. In short, comparison groups can be defined in terms of any important subject characteristic that may be relevant to intellectual behavior and that is outside the experimenter's control. "Important" is of course a vague descriptor; in our view, an "important" characteristic is one that is relevant not simply to incidental aspects of a few tasks (for example, color blindness) but across a wide range of everyday situations (literacy, for instance).

For every specific area of comparative research there are specific methodological problems. Comparisons across cultural groups, for example, raise concerns about whether the experimenter's questions, formulated in one language, convey the same meaning to members of other language groups. But in a more subtle way, the same problem arises when experimenters use the same kind of questions with children and adults. The assumption underlying this book is that most of the specific difficulties associated with various research specialties are in fact instances of several general classes of problems in method and interpretation that are part of the very nature of comparative cognitive research. In future chapters we will discuss these difficulties as well as some strategies for coping with them. But first we would like to offer some thoughts on why researchers decide to conduct comparative studies in the first place.

Over the years, comparative cognitive research has been stimulated by a variety of interests. Developmental, cross-cultural, and social-class comparisons, for instance, have all appealed to a desire to understand the mental processes of human adults in industrialized societies through comparison and contrast with members of other groups. Historically, this interest was originally predicated on the notion of evolution. The adult developed from the child, *Homo sapiens* and the primates both evolved from a common ancestor, and modern industrial cultures developed from early tribal societies. The premise behind what Medin and Cole (1975) have called the "search for historical antecedents" is that subjects who are younger, of another species, or from a less technologically advanced culture share certain basic characteristics with Western man's predecessors along a scale of ontogenetic, phylogenetic, or cultural evolution. The assumption is made that characteristics that separate adults in a technological society from various comparison groups (such as language acquisition, the development of opposed thumbs for tool grasping, or the invention of a writing system) may be examined as potential causal factors for the modern adult's cognitive abilities. Although this approach has been generally discredited as a means of demonstrating causation, it has played an important role in stimulating interest in the study of comparative cognition.

In a more pragmatic vein, comparative research has been of value because it allows us to study the effects associated with different values of interesting variables that are beyond experimental control. Since age, culture, and species are associated with obvious gross differences among individuals, it is natural that researchers should want to investigate the differences in cognitive processes that might be associated with these gross differences.

Further, comparative studies offer potential benefits in developing and refining hypotheses about cognition, regardless of whether there is an accompanying interest in studying the comparison groups in their own right. For example, developmental psychologists have been interested in the role that increasing experience with language in general, and with the term *why* in particular, might play in the child's ability to understand causal relationships. Although the researcher cannot seriously entertain the notion of taking a random sample of infants and isolating them from language, it is possible to study causal reasoning in deaf children. Research with special groups can also aid the scientist seeking to disentangle certain variables that are usually confounded within our own society. Age and formal schooling, for instance, are two variables that are associated with large differences in cognitive functioning but that increase together both in our own culture and in most technological societies. Studying children in countries where formal schooling is not universal and does not begin at any specific age is one strategy for trying to assess the individual contributions of these two factors.

The desire to test the adequacy and generality of a hypothesis is another reason for conducting comparative research. If pressed to justify his research plans, Roger Brown's graduate student would probably offer a dubious argument about the need to test the generality of the effects he has obtained with educated adults. There is little point in testing the generality of a "mini-theory" that applies to just a narrow range of tasks or that has been corroborated in only a handful of studies with the standard population. But a theory of major scope and importance merits tests of its generality, particularly when the theory contains implications about universal principles in cognitive functioning. The body of cross-cultural research testing the generality of Jean Piaget's stages of cognitive development across wide variations in cultural and experiential background is a prominent example of comparative studies that have been used in evaluating an important general theory.

In recent decades, government and society at large have increasingly pressured social scientists to pursue research that will provide answers to important social problems. This pressure has been part of a general outcry for what is termed "accountability." If society is going to support the social scientist's work, the government tells us, the scientist has an obligation to conduct research that will benefit society. The federal government has made this outlook explicit in its budget analysis: "Research and development is not . . . a separately programmed or budgeted activity of the Federal Government. Its funding must be considered in light of the potential contributions of science and technology to meeting agency or national goals and not as an end in itself" (Executive Office of the President, *Budget, 1978*, p. 290). Basic research without any readily apparent practical benefits has a hard time attracting funding in this atmosphere. The same viewpoint concerning the proper nature of government-funded research is demonstrated more flamboyantly by Senator William Proxmire's Golden Fleece awards. We would suggest that it is the lack of any obvious practical applications that makes those social science research projects he chooses to "honor" look trivial in the senator's eyes.

This demand for accountability has several effects on the nature of the research that social scientists conduct. First, the type of subjects and issues to be investigated may be determined by social, rather than theoretical, concerns. In the 1960s social science researchers responded to the sense of urgent need for measures that would ameliorate the effects of racial discrimination and poverty. The needs of the inner-city child were deemed of paramount importance and a great deal of comparative research was stimulated by this concern. In the 1970s the focus became more diffuse, and other special groups, including retarded individuals, the learning disabled, the handicapped, drug addicts, and the aged, began to receive large shares of social and governmental attention. Since that time social equity — providing all members of society with some basic level of educational and economic opportunity — has been a guiding principle for governmental programs. This principle has turned attention to the plight of groups of people deemed to be most in need. In effect, a series of comparison groups has been defined. In many cases, their difficulties are presumed to include some handicap in cognitive performance when compared to the standard population of middle-class children or adults.

In addition, the fact that the ultimate aim of the research from society's viewpoint is to produce tangible benefits in terms of general improvements in intellectual functioning has an impact on the way in which researchers frame their studies as well as the kinds of conclusions they draw. A detailed description of the behavior of subjects in a narrow set of laboratory tasks may be important in terms of a particular theory, but it will not provide legislators and bureaucrats with much insight into the kinds of training and educational programs that should be made available. The researcher often feels pressured, therefore, to couch his findings in terms of differences between groups in the use of general cognitive processes (such as "memory" or "ability to think abstractly"). A discussion of educational or remedial implications of the research is frequently considered necessary also, despite the huge gap between the narrow set of research findings and the sweeping reforms that are advocated.

These twin concerns, for accountability and for the needs of special groups, have had a major impact on the nature of federal grants and, generally, on the employment market for social scientists. Commenting on federal support for research, Richard Atkinson, Director of the National Science Foundation, has noted: "A look at government funding for science over the last decade makes it clear that applied research has been reasonably well funded while support for basic research has plummeted. To be precise, the number of dollars (adjusted for inflation) spent on applied research has increased about 2% from 1967 to the present. During the same period, funding for basic research in all fields of science has declined about

20%; in psychology the decline has been over 35%, and 25% in sociology" (Atkinson, 1977, p. 208). The Carter administration has expressed concern over the decline of basic research in this country, and the administration's 1980 budget request shows a modest effort to reverse that decline. But the increased funding for basic research is focused on non-social-science disciplines. The National Science Foundation budget request, for example, includes an increase of only 8.5 percent for the behavioral and neural sciences — where most of the foundation's funds for basic psychological research are located. In light of the current inflation rate, this increase represents no real gain for basic research in psychology.

On the employment side, Boneau and Circa (1974) commented on the results of a 1972 American Psychological Association (APA) survey: "A real prospect exists that academic jobs in departments of psychology will constitute a smaller job market than has recently obtained for new Ph.D.s . . . Of interest is the fact that the employment problem may be ameliorated by the increasing tendency of psychologists to be employed in social problem areas as a result of public policy efforts at the federal, state, and local levels, for example in health programs and in criminal justice reform" (p. 821). Of the 21,210 psychologists holding a doctorate who responded to the APA survey, 56 percent were then working in universities, medical schools, or four-year colleges. The proportion of psychologists working in basic-research positions appears to be diminishing, however, if our informal classification of job listings in the November 1977 issue of the APA *Monitor* is an indication. Of 364 different positions listed for doctorate-level psychologists, only 43 percent could be classified as academic or basic-research jobs. The remainder, as in the 1972 APA survey, were largely clinical positions, and these often specifically mentioned involvement in work with alcoholics, drug addicts, or developmentally disabled persons. Moreover, these percentages underestimate the number of psychologists doing research in applied settings because many of those in academic posts are conducting studies in such applied fields as school psychology, vocational rehabilitation, or social welfare. The figures for psychologists who are specifically trained for research positions show this trend even more clearly. A survey of psychologists who completed psychology research training programs supported by the National Institute of Mental Health (NIMH) between 1968 and 1972 found 72 percent of them in academic positions shortly after completing their training. A comparable survey of psychologists who completed programs from mid-1976 to 1978 found only 48 percent in academic posts (Schneider, 1979).

Hence, it seems reasonable to suggest that more and more researchers are working in applied areas, many of which are essentially comparative. They are expected to define, and to provide blueprints for remedying, the deficits of the mentally retarded, learning-disabled, or economically disadvantaged person. And many find themselves trying to conduct comparative research in an applied setting after having been trained in the use of methods developed in the restricted environment of the laboratory over decades of research with college sophomores. Though perfectly appropriate for many purposes, such research methods are inadequate to meet the demands of comparative research problems. The methodological problems of comparative research, severe to begin with, are increased when the researcher must not only be responsible for applied as well as theoretical conclusions but must also face strong pressures to go beyond the data to draw conclusions that are deemed relevant to policy.

This book was stimulated by our concern for the needs of the professional researcher, trained in standard experimental research, who finds himself working in an area of comparative research, as well as by concern for the student currently being trained to carry out such research. Although aimed mostly at basic comparative research, the material presented here is also relevant to those working on applied problems. Applied research, moreover, is especially likely to encounter problems of design and interpretation. Therefore we recommend that readers with a particular interest in this area also read some of the sources aimed exclusively at presenting designs and analyses of applied studies, including those in which experimental control is impossible (Campbell and Stanley, 1963; Cook and Campbell, 1976).

In chapter 2 we review the basic logic of the experimental method and its application in investigating the effects of treatment variables when questions about differences between subject groups are not at issue. This description of noncomparative research serves as a point of departure for chapter 3, which discusses the extra considerations and problems entailed in conducting and interpreting comparative studies. Chapters 4 and 5 present a series of strategies or models for comparative research and a discussion of their similarities and differences as well as their respective strengths and weaknesses. In chapter 6 we return to a consideration of the difficulties a researcher faces when working in an applied setting or trying to draw concrete implications from basic research. Although we feel that the first requirement for drawing reasonable prescriptions is that the research be based on a sound experimental model (the concern of chapters 4 and 5), the issues involved in generating practical applications from experimental studies go beyond those of sound comparative research design, and chapter 6 focuses on some of these additional problems. Finally, the appendix deals with issues of measurement and statistical analysis that are frequently encountered in conducting comparative research.

Our general approach will be to illustrate both the problems endemic to comparative studies and the strategies for coping with them, using actual research from the psychological literature. When we have described studies in order to illustrate the impact of a particular difficulty in comparative research, we have attempted to select real experiments that offer reasonable attempts at answering the question posed. We have also sought studies that are representative of comparative cognitive research in general, that are readily available in standard academic journals, and that deal with currently popular, familiar topics. It should be emphasized that our illustrations have been chosen not because they were poorly designed but because they demonstrate general problems of interpretation that are common in comparative cognitive research, even in the best of circumstances.

Both the comparative and the cognitive aspects of the type of research under discussion create problems for the investigator. When the researcher goes beyond explicit descriptions of observable behaviors in specific contexts to draw inferences about general underlying processes, he risks drawing invalid conclusions. Many different internal processes can lead to the same behavioral outcome. The major challenge for cognitive research is to design experiments that yield measures of the processes giving rise to performance and that rule out at least the most plausible rival hypotheses about the processes involved. When the researcher hypothesizes about processes going on in the heads of any subject group, he is running inferential risks that are dealt with as part of the standard training in experimental psychology. If he tries to draw conclusions about the different processes going on in two different groups, he is of course compounding his risks. He will have a very difficult time ascribing a difference in performance to any particular variable — let alone to the underlying process it is presumed to affect. Because the two comparison groups differ in a host of ways, it will be logically impossible even to maintain that theresearcher's treatment is psychologically identical for both. Hence, it should not be surprising that so many inferences about group differences in mental processes based on differential performance in psychological experiments and tests have been the cause for intense controversy. The problem is that such inferences, especially when intuitively plausible or attractive, have in a number of instances gained widespread acceptance before the advent of more fine-grained research could challenge their validity. Problems are especially likely to arise when studies deal with concepts, such as intelligence, environmental stimulation, or socioeconomic status, that frequently are not rigorously defined but are likely to turn up in research having "practical" implications. Such a state of affairs clearly poses a problem for social scientists, who have to make life-affecting decisions about people; no clear prescriptions are possible on the basis of weak and conflicting evidence. Invalid inferences also present risks for society, especially in a climate where social science research is supported in part because of its usefulness in supplying a basis for political decision-making.

While it is not our intent to argue against practical recommendations based on comparative research, we do want to underscore the need for extreme caution. The researcher risks error when: (1) he goes beyond the behavior observed under a particular set of circumstances to hypothesize about general cognitive processes; (2) he tries to interpret differences in performance manifested by groups that vary in unspecified but certainly numerous ways; and (3) he extrapolates from research on a narrow range of tasks in controlled settings to the world at large. Practical prescriptions based on comparative cognitive research suffer from all three of these very important threats to their validity. This book will call attention to such risks and offer some guidelines for trying to reduce their magnitude. But where the potential social impact is large, there will always be a need for extreme caution and for many studies deliberately designed to bridge the chasm between experimental research and practical application.

2.

The Normative Logic of Experimental Design

There are good reasons for beginning this book on comparative cognitive research with a review of the accepted logic of noncomparative, experimental research. First, an analysis of the logic of noncomparative experimental design makes it apparent that although the typical comparative study superficially resembles its noncomparative counterpart—the two types of study are written up in the same format and are often published in the same journals—the comparative study does not meet even the most basic assumption of standard experimental design. Second, when predictions concerning a theoretical construct that refers to a cognitive process are tested, the logic of experimentation may become complex. The ensuing difficulties, as well as the basic strategy for coping with them by developing and testing a theoretical model through a series of studies, can best be introduced within the framework of noncomparative research, where the complicating factors entailed in developing multiple models to fit the differing functioning of multiple subject groups need not be considered.

The basic steps in a program of experimental research as practiced by contemporary psychologists are diagrammed in figure 2.1.[1]

The researcher specifies a phenomenon embodied in a cognitive task. The list of phenomena that could be studied is, of

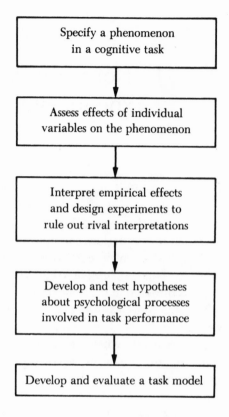

Figure 2.1. Basic steps in a standard experimental research program.

course, endless. Particular behavioral events may be chosen as research topics for various reasons: because of their importance in relation to existing theory, for practical purposes, or simply out of curiosity about some aspect of human functioning. The only restrictions are that the researcher must be able to reliably produce or uncover the phenomenon and must be able to describe it objectively so that other observers can agree on its presence or absence in a given situation.[2] (A detailed discussion of the nature and importance of such objective descriptions of phenomena is available in many sources, including Underwood, 1957, pp. 51-84.)

A much-studied phenomenon taken from the literature on human memory will illustrate the components of an experimental research program. This phenomenon involves the way in which people organize individual items in a free recall task. In such a task, subjects are presented with a list of words, one at a time, and afterwards try to recall them in any order they like. Bousfield (1953) found that when the word list is composed of instances selected from four taxonomic categories (animals, names, professions, vegetables), subjects do not recall the words in the order in which they have been presented, but tend to recall together items from the same category. Bousfield termed this effect *clustering*. Ever since he called attention to it, this phenomenon has been the target of a vast number of research studies, a few of which will be cited in illustrating the remaining steps in a program of experimental research.

The researcher begins assessing the effects that individual variables have on the phenomenon. To test each variable, he randomly assigns subjects to groups and administers a different treatment to each group. In the simplest case—that involving two groups—the basic strategy is to measure the performance of one group of subjects in the presence of some specified amount of the variable of interest (say, the opportunity to study each word on a free recall list for four seconds) and then to compare this group's performance with that of a second group receiving a different amount (or none) of the variable under test. (The second group might receive the same list of words with eight seconds of study time for each word). If this comparison is to be interpretable, the researcher must be sure that the two groups of subjects were comparable before he introduced the treatment variable. If one group was more knowledgeable, motivated, or fatigued than the other, differences in performance could not be attributed to the difference in experimental treatment. The most acceptable strategy for obtaining equivalence is through random assignment of subjects to treatment groups. If the level of the treatment variable that any particular subject receives is determined on a chance basis, on the average, subjects in two treatment groups of adequate size will be comparable in terms of all subject characteristics; that is, in the long run, the two groups will contain about the same number of bright people, anxious people, tall people, left-handed people, and so on.[3] Because any subject variable could conceivably be related to performance on the experimental task, this construction of equivalent groups through random assignment is a critical feature of the experimental method.

Besides making sure that the two treatment groups are composed of comparable subjects, the experimenter must also ensure that the two groups are treated alike in all respects, with the exception of the single variable under test. All extraneous features of the experimental treatment and the testing environment (all features not being tested) must be equated for the two groups. In another example from the literature on free recall clustering, when Cofer, Bruce, and Reicher (1966) wanted to assess the effect of lumping together items from the same category on the study list (for example, "leopard, tiger, zebra . . .") as opposed to positioning them randomly, they had to handle groups alike with respect to other aspects of the task. For instance, the two groups received the same set of words, the same instructions, the same pacing for the study trial, and the same time for recall. Holding extraneous task and environmental variables constant in this manner is one of the major methods of ensuring that groups are treated equivalently (except with regard to the variable being tested). When it is not practical for researchers to hold a particular extraneous variable constant, or when they are interested in demonstrating that this one does not interact with the variable under study, they may vary the extraneous variable systematically, balancing the two groups with respect to the proportion of subjects experiencing each level of the variable. For example, if practical constraints dictate the use of more than one experimenter in a study, the approved procedure is to have each experimenter administer the task to an equal proportion of subjects in each treatment group.

In addition, an unspecifiable number of miscellaneous variables that are associated with the treatment or testing environment, such as the level of noise outside the testing room or the room temperature, will be difficult, expensive, or impossible to control or systematically vary. The equation of treatment groups in terms of such miscellaneous factors can be achieved through the same procedure of random assignment of subjects to treatments as is used to ensure that subjects in the different treatment groups are comparable prior to treatment. If the particular treatment a subject receives when he arrives at the testing room is determined through a random assignment process, then not only subject characteristics but also the time of testing and miscellaneous variations in the environment will be equated, on the average, for the various treatment groups.

The researcher interprets the empirically demonstrated effects. Scientists are not satisfied with demonstrating that a certain operationally defined manipulation produces a change in performance (for example, that putting items from the same category on a recall list leads to better performance than giving subjects "noncategorizable" words). The deeper question concerns the interpretation of the manipulation and the description of the resulting effect in theoretical terms. In the studies of free recall clustering, the fact that words selected from the same category tend to be recalled together is generally accepted as an empirical fact. The issue of which theoretical variable is being manipulated when list words are selected from the same or from different categories is more controversial. Generally, the implicit assumption is that the construct being manipulated is categorical relatedness. Some have maintained, however, that the critical variable is interword association—that words selected from the same category are recalled together not because they are categorically related but because they are commonly thought of in association with one another or in a common context (for example, "table" and "chair," or "leopard" and "tiger"). Clustering can then be construed as the result of manipulating interitem association rather than category membership. Moreover, Jenkins and his associates have shown that a recall list composed of items selected from norms for words that are frequently associated with one another will produce more recall and clustering than lists composed of words that are not commonly associated with one another (Jenkins and Russell, 1952; Jenkins, Mink, and Russell, 1958). The problem is that category membership and degree of association tend to vary together. Just as Bousfield's category instances were sometimes associatively related, Jenkins' verbal associates were often members of a common category. In order to establish which of these two variables was producing the clustering phenomenon, researchers sought to compose recall lists in such a way that the two variables could be separated (Bousfield and Puff, 1964; Cofer, 1965; Marshall, 1967; Wood and Underwood, 1967). All of this research, however, has not succeeded in ruling out either variable in favor of the other. Clustering does occur for associatively related words that are not members of a common category, but the effect is more pronounced for words that are related in both of these ways (Cofer, 1966). Thus, experimental methods provide procedures for using a single experiment to demonstrate the effect of some operationally defined manipulation, but they do not tell how to identify that manipulation in theoretical terms.

The researcher develops and tests hypotheses about the psychological processes involved in task performance. Assumptions about the meaning of a manipulation in theoretical terms are closely related to the experimenter's hypotheses about the cognitive processes responsible for a phenomenon. Unfortunately, the involvement of a particular process in performing some task cannot be demonstrated in the same way as the effect of some operationally defined manipulation. We cannot observe and directly manipulate cognitive processes, such as mentally organizing a recall list in terms of a prior knowledge of categories, in the way that we manipulate task variables (such as the arrangement of words on the study list) to see if they affect performance. Therefore, the researcher's hypotheses about these internal processes have to be tested in another way, according to the following logic. A hypothetical causal process P is assumed to be activated when the subject performs the task under study. The researcher tries to devise some condition that, if P is operating, should produce a specifiable change in the phenomenon. This condition is instituted, and if the predicted outcome is observed, the researcher proceeds on the working assumption that his or her explanation is correct and goes on to test additional predictions based on the hypothesis that P is involved in task performance. The enterprise is complicated by the fact that although such a positive result is consistent with the hypothesis that P is involved in task performance, it does not rule out other explanations. Because different underlying processes may lead to the same observable behaviors, any one of a number of processes could logically be responsible for the predicted outcome. However, if a process hypothesis leads to a prediction under some condition and that outcome is *not* obtained, that process explanation can be ruled out of contention.[4] Theoretically, then, experiments have greater power in eliminating incorrect hypotheses than they do in proving true ones. The attempt to establish causal explanations becomes an effort to design experiments in such a way as to produce results that are consistent with a favored process hypothesis and that at the same time rule out prominent rival explanations.

The controversy over the interpretation of clustering effects was related to rival conceptions of the processes involved in free recall. Researchers who conceptualized memory as a process of organizing or "unitizing" disparate items into larger and larger units emphasized the category membership variable. Taxonomic categories provide convenient higher-level units, and instances of the same category are presumably recalled together because the subject first remembers the category (for example, professions) and then its members (dentist, farmer, judge). Other researchers disputed this organizational theory of recall processes and stressed the view that memory is based on the association of contiguous items. A category name and its instances are associated with each other as a result of frequent contiguity in real-world contexts. In a free recall task, members of a taxonomic category are recalled contiguously more often than are unrelated words because when a category instance appears on the study list, the subject thinks of the category name associated with it and also of any other list words associated with that name (for example, "leopard" — animal — horse). Thus, category instances are rehearsed together by virtue of their common association with the category name.

Employing the strategy just described for corroborating an explanatory hypothesis, Wood and Underwood (1967) reasoned that if the association hypothesis was correct and the previously seen category members are implicitly rehearsed each time a new member of the category appears on the study list, the category instances appearing early on a study list should have a higher probability of being recalled than those appearing later. In testing this prediction, Wood and Underwood wanted to be able to control the implicit associations that subjects would have between list words. They used words that were members of color categories (such as "canary," "sulphur," "custard") because subjects do not give a common word association to them unless they are told to limit their responses to sense impressions. To elicit the category names as implicit responses for one group of subjects, a colored patch corresponding to the relevant color category was shown after each word. Other groups saw inappropriate color patches or no patches. As predicted, probability of recall was inversely related to study list position for subjects who received appropriate category cues but not for those who received inappropriate cues or no cues. Thus, Wood and Underwood garnered support for the hypothesis that subjects implicitly rehearse list members that are associated with the same category label as the current list item. However, obtaining the predicted outcome does not rule out all other process explanations. For instance, the following organizational explanation of the Wood and Underwood results might be given. Subjects require several trials to organize the study list completely. On the initial trial, they tend to use the first items they receive from each category to set up their organization of the list. Therefore, when Wood and Underwood tested recall after a single trial, their subjects responded largely with the first few items from each category because later items were not yet integrated into their list organization. Thus it should be apparent that demonstrating the truth of a process explanation is not nearly so straightforward a matter as showing that an operationally defined manipulation produces an effect on performance. No single experiment will rule out all plausible alternative hypotheses. Over a series of studies, however, the researcher does try to rule out those rival process hypotheses that have emerged and to demonstrate that his process theory accounts for the largest body of data.

The researcher may develop an explicit model of task performance. To understand an intellectual task fully, whether it is free recall, prose comprehension, or basic addition, the researcher needs to ascertain not only what cognitive processes are relevant but also how the various component processes are combined to produce performance. To understand free recall, for example, we must know more than just that the process of organization is involved. We need to know at what point and how the list words are organized, as well as how the organizational process fits in with other processes, such as rehearsal and retrieval. Models of the way in which processes are combined to yield task performance may vary considerably in amount of detail and in explicitness, but they have in common the attempt to provide an account of all the factors included in performance rather than merely to specify that some single factor is relevant. One example of an informal model is the organizational model of free recall developed by Mandler (1967). Mandler's theoretical model, which goes beyond the general principle that subjects organize list words into larger units that are accessed and then "unpacked" at recall, hypothesizes how the subject might develop these larger units over a series of trials with the same list: "Recall after the first trial probably reflects category recall, that is, approximately one word from a large proportion of the categories. On subsequent trials these categories are then 'filled up' with items up to the capacity of 5 ± 2. Given a constant number of categories, the optimal strategy might be to add one item to each category on each trial" (p. 367).

Although this model has not been tested in its entirety, Mandler and his associates have done research that supports various portions of it. For instance, the notion that the subject will tend to learn one new item for each of his categories on each study trial leads to the testable prediction that the number of words a subject recalls will be largely a function of the number of categories he uses to organize the recall list. To test this prediction, Mandler needed to vary and to measure the number of categories that subjects use to structure a recall list. He wanted also to ensure that all subjects actually had organized the recall list before they were tested on it. A variant of the clustering paradigm was developed to meet these requirements. Subjects were given word lists that did not have any ostensible category structure and were then instructed to sort the list any way they liked into not more than seven groupings. Subjects sorted the same list on repeated trials until they arrived at exactly identical groupings on two consecutive trials. After each subject had achieved this stable sort, his recall was tested; and it turned out that, as predicted, recall was a function of the number of groupings the subject had used to sort the list (Mandler and Pearlstone, 1966; Mandler, 1967).

In recent years a number of cognitive psychologists have begun to provide more explicit, detailed performance models, often called "task analyses," of the activities that go on covertly in the course of an experiment. These models may consist of a detailed listing of the steps involved in executing the task, a mathematical formula integrating performance parameters, or a computer program designed to simulate human performance. One such computer program is called FRAN (the acronym for Free Recall in an Associative Net), a model of free recall performance developed by Anderson and Bower (1972). This model will be described in detail in order to provide a general picture of what a task performance model is like and the way its validity is tested. Despite the apparent complexity of this enterprise, the creators of the model recognize it as a severe simplification. FRAN is based on a conception of human memory as a permanent associative network with nodes corresponding to individual words. An association consists of two word nodes (for example, the nodes representing "jewel" and "diamond") plus a label indicating the type of relationship existing between them (superordinate-subordinate). In the computer model, this hypothetical network is represented by a net of 262 nouns. The model also includes a short-term memory store representing up to five items that have been heard of or thought about very recently, as well as a mechanism called ENTRYSET that functions in a recall task as a repository for a few list words that become directly associated with the recall list (that is, whenever the subject thinks of "the list I learned first," he immediately thinks of a few words from it).

In a free recall task, a word on the study list enters the short-term store (STS) and is "tagged" (with a specifiable probability) as a member of that particular list. In the process of studying this word, FRAN follows associative pathways connecting it to other word nodes to see if any of those words are items that have been seen already on the recall list. This process is illustrated in figure 2.2. Each boxed word represents a node in the associative net, the arrows represent associations between nodes, and each × represents a list tag. When the word "mother" appears on the study list, it is put in short-term store and the node representing "mother" is tagged as an item on the current recall list. As indicated in figure 2.2A,[5] FRAN then moves out from this node to seek words associated with "mother" that are also on the list. In this fashion, FRAN examines the node representing the word "house." Because "house" has already been tagged as an item on the list, the pathways in both directions between "mother" and "house" are given list tags, as in figure 2.2B. Returning to "mother," FRAN tries another pathway, checking "baby" for list membership. Because, in our example, "baby" has already been checked once and not found on the list, FRAN proceeds to check a second-order association, "doll," which is found to be a list item. Consequently, the paths connecting "mother" and

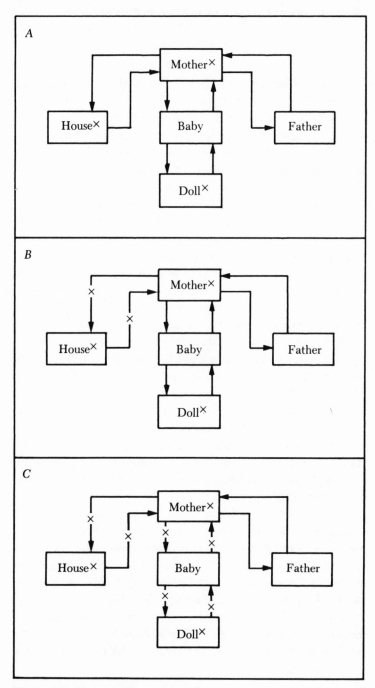

Figure 2.2. Free recall in an associative net. Adapted from J. R. Anderson, 1972, vol. 5, figs. 2 and 4.

"baby" and those between "baby" and "doll" are tagged, as in figure 2.2C.

At recall, these tagged associative pathways will guide the search for list words. FRAN first produces the items currently in short-term store (usually the last five items on the study list) and then begins with an item from short-term store or ENTRYSET and works through the tagged associative pathways leading out from that word's node to search for additional list words. FRAN's recall process can be illustrated by returning to figure 2.2C and using "mother" as a sample entry word. First, FRAN proceeds along the tagged pathway from "mother" to "house." Since "house" is marked as a list word, FRAN produces it as a response. There are no further tagged pathways leading out from "house"; so FRAN returns to "mother" and follows the tagged pathway to "baby." "Baby" is not marked as a list word; so FRAN does not produce it but follows the tagged pathway to "doll," which is tagged as a list item and consequently is recalled. This procedure of following each tagged pathway out as far as it goes and then returning to the node representing "mother" to look for another tagged pathway is repeated until all the tagged paths from "mother" are exhausted. (In our example, FRAN does not follow the pathway from "mother" to "father" because it does not have a list tag.) After exploring all the tagged pathways leading out from "mother," FRAN moves to another entry word and proceeds in the same fashion.

FRAN's complexity — the number of component processes and the assumptions on which they are based — is dictated by the need to model the recall process in sufficient detail so that a computer can actually produce recall protocols. The model is not tested piece by piece but in its entirety. While the logic of the usual experimental test of a causal hypothesis is summed up as "If process P, then outcome O," the logic of model testing is more like "If processes P, Q, R, S, and T, under assumptions A, B, C, and D, then outcome O." Rather than setting up two treatment conditions, which are hypothesized to affect process *P* differently, the model-testing approach involves having the model and human subjects generate outcomes independently under the same treatment condition. The basic problem in model testing is that most of the individual component processes humans employ in a task (in our example, free recall) are not measured, and therefore cannot be directly compared with the model's processes. If FRAN and humans produce different kinds of output (perform at different levels or respond differently to some change in treatment), we do not know what step in the modeled process is involved. For example, human subjects show greater recall and clustering than FRAN on categorized word lists, especially with blocked presentation (Anderson, 1972). The knowledge that the recall of humans differs from that of FRAN in this situation does not, however, reveal the particular memory structure or step in the recall process that is the source of the difference. FRAN incorporates several structures (a short-term store or STS, ENTRYSET, and the associative net itself) and literally dozens of component processing steps.

Tentative flow diagrams of the steps involved in FRAN are given in figures 2.3-2.5. Figure 2.3 shows the study processes used by FRAN. While words are being studied, FRAN also goes through a number of steps in order to update ENTRYSET, as illustrated in figure 2.4. Finally, when directed to recall the list, FRAN executes the retrieval processes shown in figure 2.5. If these diagrams accomplish nothing else, they at least indicate the complexity of a simulation model for even a "simple" cognitive task such as free recall. Any one of the structures or processing steps or any combination of them could be the source of differences between FRAN and humans in recall performance. Moreover, in the case of categorized list recall, a good number of the steps in FRAN constitute not just possible but highly plausible alternative sources of performance differences.

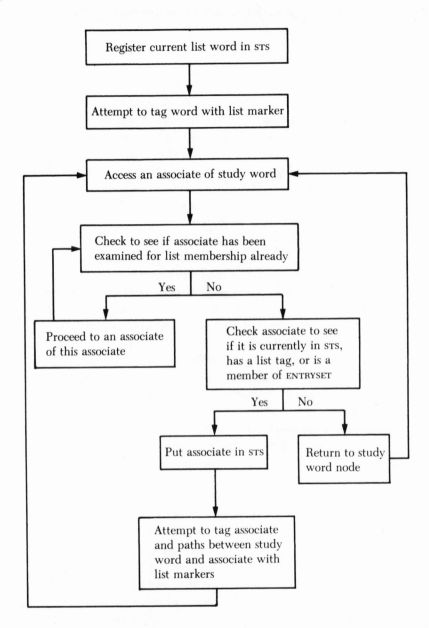

Figure 2.3. Study processes in Anderson and Bower's model of free recall (FRAN). The study process for an individual word is hypothesized to include checking five associates plus one additional associate for each second of study time and to be terminated by the onset of the next word on the recall list. This and figures 2.4 and 2.5 are based on the model presented in J. R. Anderson, 1972, vol. 5.

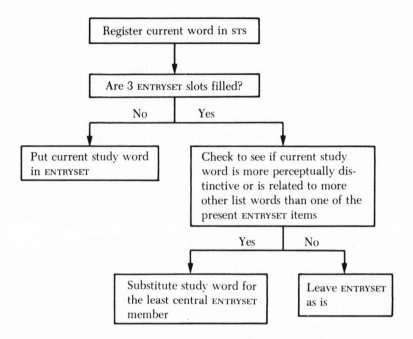

Figure 2.4. Updating ENTRYSET in FRAN. The updating takes place concurrently with the study processes depicted in figure 2.3.

Humans may differ from FRAN in several respects: (1) in having varying probabilities of tagging words as list items, depending on the type of word being studied (for example, being more likely to associate a word with the list context if it is a member of the same category as an earlier list word); (2) in giving preference, when a word is studied, to checking associative pathways representing superordinate relationships (that is, being more likely to look for a word that is a member of the same category as "mother" rather than to look for words such as "house" that are associated with "mother" in other ways); (3) in using different rules for selecting retrieval "routes" through the associative network (for example, testing all members of a

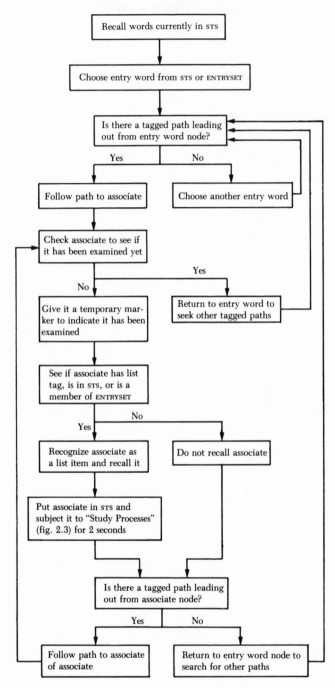

Figure 2.5. Retrieval processes in FRAN. When all STS and ENTRYSET items have been used as entry words, recall ceases.

category before exploring other associates of any given member); or (4) in using different criteria for choosing entry words, perhaps including the use of category names even though they are not list words. A model such as FRAN is useful because it constitutes a complete, explicit theory of the task. In the many situations where FRAN and humans perform very similarly, FRAN offers a viable hypothesis concerning the component processes in recall. But where the model's output differs from that of humans (as with categorized lists), such tests of the model do not reveal the sources of these differences. Moreover, when it is a matter of comparing different subject groups, if a given model's output matches the performance of one group but not that of another, it seems clear that we are still far from solving the problem of isolating the particular cognitive process that is the locus of group differences.

It is evident, even from this simplified discussion of standard experimental methods, that in three distinctive ways these methods are set apart from those employed in comparative studies.

First, there is the question of the goals of the research. Our descriptions of some of the clustering studies show that standard experimental research is concerned with constructing what might be called "a theory of the task." The subject population is held constant and some treatment variable is manipulated to see what effect it has on clustering. In a sense, the focus of interest is the phenomenon per se, not the characteristics of the subjects. Comparative research has the opposite goal. It holds the task constant and varies the subject population to see how differences among subjects affect performance. Even the simple two-group comparison is aimed at a "theory of the subject." We believe, however — as later chapters of this book will make clear — that comparative cognitive psychology must be based on the union of a theory of the task with a theory of the subject. It is impossible to understand the differences between people that lead to different performances without first understanding the component processes of the task eliciting those performances.

The second characteristic of standard experiments is their reliance on the use of random assignment of subjects to treatment conditions. This procedure is crucial in guaranteeing the internal validity of an experiment, that is, that groups are equivalent except for the variation in a single treatment variable, which can therefore be regarded as the cause for any group differences in performance. Random assignment is necessary to ensure that the two groups will be equivalent, on the average, in terms of the characteristics of subjects and also in terms of irrelevant variables linked to the particular occasion on which a subject is tested. When groups are determined by nature rather than by random assignment, these guarantees do not hold.

Third, the standard research method has benefited from the fact that experimenters have undertaken such studies with a great deal of knowledge about their subjects, both in the form of previous research results and in the more implicit knowledge stemming from shared cultural and environmental backgrounds. Having such information, the experimenters could begin their testing with a fair degree of confidence that their subjects — all of whom were college students — would interpret a given set of instructions as intended, that they would exhibit reasonable levels of recall on a list of a certain length, and that words selected from standard category norms would in fact be considered instances of the relevant categories by the subjects in the recall study. This point is crucial to the whole logic of the clustering paradigm, which presumes that the experimenter can specify the subject's organizational categories (or categorical associations) in advance. The paradigm makes sense only if the categories set up by researchers are those generally available to, and employed by, the subjects. Assumptions such as these, based on previous research and on familiarity with the subjects, become tenuous in comparative studies.

These last two differences between comparative and standard research mean that the comparative researcher's task is complicated in some very fundamental ways. The factors that safeguard the internal validity of a standard experiment do not function in comparative studies. Thus the comparative researcher needs to develop more complex, cautious methods, and to be wary of making spurious inferences about group differences, as we will see in the chapters that follow.

3.

What Happens When All Other Things Are Not Equal?

In noncomparative cognitive research, different versions of a task (such as free recall) are presented to equivalent or randomly assigned groups of subjects, and researchers try to see how the variations they introduce affect performance. Although it is common to speak of this as research about psychological *processes*, we have emphasized that this kind of research produces a theory of the task, or, in other words, an understanding of the relevant variables that influence performance in specifiable ways. In the extended example given in chapter 2, the performances being considered were category clustering and number of words recalled.

But what is the logic of the research enterprise when we do not have equivalent groups — when, in fact, we do not *want* to have equivalent groups because we are interested in how different groups recall words, or engage in some other cognitive task? In common parlance, our interest lies in group differences in the way people think. The research we engage in may be motivated by an interest in proving a theoretical point about a widely used psychological task. More often it will be motivated by an interest in the nature of psychological differences between groups, differences in what may be called abilities, motives, or understanding. Whatever the motivation for beginning an experiment on groups that are manifestly different in ways related to the task, there is one inescapable consequence: we will violate the logic that permits valid inferences from the kinds of studies reviewed in chapter 2.

Because we cannot randomly assign subjects to treatments when the "treatment" is age, culture, or species, we cannot ensure that groups are equivalent in terms of all factors except the one we are investigating. On the contrary, comparison groups will generally be vastly different in terms of a large number of characteristics relating to widely divergent past experiences, or to physiological differences, or to a combination of the two. Different age groups, for example, differ not only in chronological age but also in amount and type of schooling, specific knowledge, exposure to certain types of testing situations, physical dexterity, and neural development. Different cultural groups may differ in terms of language, rearing patterns, type of educational experience, the value placed on different personal and cognitive qualities, and physical health. "Age" and "culture" are merely blanket labels that conveniently cover a host of differences that cannot be completely specified.

The "all other things being equal" assumption of the experimental method is thus violated in two ways. (1) Our comparison groups will generally differ on not one but a multitude of dimensions. Hence, we will have difficulty in proving that any one particular difference between our groups is the source of observed differences in performance. (2) We will not be able to ensure that our treatment is equivalent for different groups at all points during the experimental task. If our groups are, in a psychological sense, receiving different treatments, the interpretation of observed group differences is further clouded. Both of these problems need to be examined before we consider the general approaches that are available for comparative research.[1]

Obtaining Comparable Groups

The experimental method was designed as a technique for isolating and individually testing variables in order to demonstrate cause-effect relationships. Our inability to isolate and manipulate any single subject variable in a comparative study violates a fundamental assumption of that method and precludes attributing an experimental effect to any one aspect of the groups' differences. For instance, a sample of schizophrenic subjects might perform differently in a test of recognition memory from a sample of normal subjects—not because schizophrenia is relevant to recognition memory in and of itself but because schizophrenics happen to be (1) less educated, (2) more easily distracted, (3) less interested in doing well on the test, or (4) affected in some other way by experiences associated with living in a mental hospital. When we find a difference between such comparison groups, the fact that they differ along so many dimensions makes it difficult to pinpoint the relevant variable.

The risk entailed in automatically attributing group differences to the kinds of variables usually used to define group membership (for example, age, ethnic group, sex) can be demonstrated by referring to work that Zigler (1966) and his associates have done with mentally retarded children. Earlier research comparing the performances of retarded and normal children of the same mental age had led to the widely accepted conclusion that retarded children are more "rigid" in their behavior. This conclusion was based on such experimental findings as the greater persistence of retarded subjects in comparison to normal subjects when asked to repeat the same simple task over and over again. Zigler maintained that this persistence, which many had interpreted as a quasi-physiological mental rigidity inherent in retardation, is instead an artifact stemming from differences between the previous social experiences of the two types of children. Because of their relative deprivation in terms of previous social interaction, institutionalized retardates tend to place a higher value on the social aspects of interaction with an adult experimenter and hence to persist in a boring task in order to keep that interaction going. When Zigler examined the previous social histories of institutionalized retardates, he found that those children who had been most deprived of positive social experiences showed the most persistence in the experimental task. Further research indicated that institutionalized children with normal IQs showed as much persistence as institutionalized retardates, while retarded children who had not been institutionalized were no more persistent than their normal-IQ counterparts. Thus, a group difference in performance on a persistence task that had been attributed to differences in intellectual level appears to be more appropriately related to differences in previous social experience. When we try to "manipulate" intellectual level by comparing normal and retarded individuals, we are manipulating a whole host of other factors (such as social history) at the same time. In view of this fact, the attempt to attribute a difference between the two groups to any one subject variable is logically unfounded. Moreover, the new light that Zigler's findings shed on the nature of the subject variable that is producing the difference in persistence (social experience rather than intellectual level) brings with it a reinterpretation of the cognitive construct tapped by the experimental task (the level of motivation rather than rigidity).

The fallacy of attributing group performance differences to a single difference between groups while ignoring other potential causal factors is widespread. One finds this sort of interpretation in developmental studies, cross-cultural studies, comparisons of different psychopathological groups, and comparisons of different racial or social-class groups. Many among the recent crop of "life span" studies comparing the intellectual functioning of the elderly with that of younger subjects demonstrate the same fallacy. There has been a tendency to test a group of college or middle-aged subjects on the one hand and a group of elderly subjects (often conveniently sampled from rest homes) on the other, and then to attribute any differences in performance to mental deterioration (again, presumably physiological) accompanying old age. The problem is of course that the two groups are likely to differ not just with respect to age but also in terms of present living conditions, attained educational level, physical health, and motivation. The need to examine such correlated group differences is illustrated in a study by Mistler-Lachman (1977). Mistler-Lachman looked at age differences in memory, using an experimental paradigm called release from proactive inhibition. When college students are given repeated trials in a memory task with very similar materials (for example, digit triplets such as 723, 614, 892), their performance declines over trials. However, if they are then given a trial with a different type of material (letter trigrams such as BQD, PLX, MUK), they perform at a high level again, presumably because the inhibition generated by the digit triplets has been "released." Mistler-Lachman administered this task to elderly people selected as the most competent residents of a rest home, with the added restriction that selected subjects not have any apparent mental disabilities, and found that they did not profit from the change in stimuli as much as college students did. This sort of difference between college students and elderly subjects has often been interpreted as evidence of the onset of learning deficits in old age. Mistler-Lachman, however, did not assume that age alone was necessarily responsible for the difference between groups. She felt that factors associated with living in a rest home might be involved and therefore included a third group in her study: elderly persons living in the community. When the comparison was made between college students and these elderly persons, there was no difference in the amount of memory improvement after switching from one type of material to another. The performance of the community-based elderly thus demonstrated that the difference between college students and rest-home elderly in ability to benefit from a change in type of materials could not be attributed to age per se.

The first strategy that comes to mind for trying to rule out alternative explanations of group differences is to select comparison groups so that they are matched in terms of characteristics that are not under study (such as type of residence) but that could also produce the predicted effect. If this strategy works, as in the Mistler-Lachman example, an error of inference may be avoided. But the problem with matching is that we can never be sure it has been carried far enough. We might select elderly and young adult subjects for a comparative study in such a way that the groups were matched for years of schooling, economic class, and type of living environment.[2] However, such matching does not necessarily solve the problem of guarding against relevant but uncontrolled variables. There will be some potentially important variables on which we cannot match comparison groups. For example, in a study comparing elderly people and young adults it would be impossible to match age groups in a cross-sectional study in terms of the historical period during which they had been reared. There might be effects related to having been raised and educated in America during World War I, as opposed to during the 1950s, and we would be unable to control for these generation effects in a comparative study of age groups. Leaving aside this class of necessarily confounding variables, we can match on most variables known or suspected to be related to the dependent variable, but we can never be sure we have matched on all relevant subject characteristics. A variable on which we have failed to match comparison groups may turn out to be critical. This is not just a problem in theory but a very real pitfall repeatedly encountered in comparative research.

Cross-cultural research conducted by Berry (1968, 1971) illustrates the insufficiency of even the most diligent efforts to match subjects on potentially confounding variables. Berry's work was prompted by earlier findings on the effects of culture on visual perception. Researchers concerned with these effects had found differences between European and non-European groups in susceptibility to the Muller-Lyer illusion (shown in figure 3.1). Europeans tended to be more taken in by the illusion, that is, more likely to perceive the line with "arrow ends" as shorter than the other line (Rivers, 1901, 1905; Segall, Campbell, and Herskovitz, 1966). A widely accepted inter-

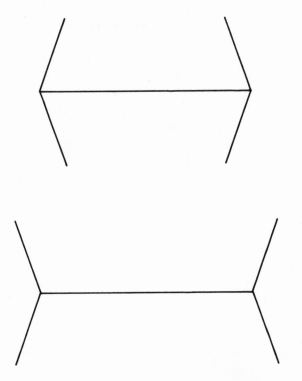

Figure 3.1. The Muller-Lyer illusion.

pretation of this cultural difference revolved around presumed differences in perceptual experience. Europeans live in "carpentered" environments characterized by straight lines, right angles, and square corners. It was hypothesized that such experiences led Europeans to see the angles formed by the intersecting lines in the Muller-Lyer figures in terms of square corners extending off into space. The environments of many of the non-European groups in these studies do not offer comparable experience in viewing rectangular figures from different angles, and the relative lack of this type of experience was presumed to be responsible for their lessened susceptibility to the illusion. However, people from European and non-European cultures differ in a vast number of ways. Later, stronger tests of the "carpenteredness" hypothesis were made by comparing people within the same cultural group who happen to live in environments varying in carpenteredness: for example, Africans living in traditional rural environments and members of the same tribal group living in African cities with European-style architecture. When this type of comparison was made, researchers often failed to find differences in susceptibility to the illusion (Jahoda, 1966).

Berry pointed out that a likely source of the discrepant findings was failure to control for differences in perceptual development. Susceptibility to the Muller-Lyer illusion diminishes with age, presumably as a result of increasing perceptual development. Although the susceptibility of Europeans or westernized non-Europeans would tend to be increased by their more carpentered environments, any advantage they might have in terms of perceptual development as compared with non-Europeans in traditional societies would act in the opposite direction, that is, to reduce their Muller-Lyer susceptibility. Berry made an attempt to disentangle these factors by comparing the Muller-Lyer performances of two subgroups within an Eskimo culture whose environments differed in carpenteredness but who were matched in terms of scores on a test of perceptual development (as well as on age and sex). With these controls, Berry found a significant effect for carpenteredness of environment within the Eskimo culture. However, it turned out that he had not been careful enough in matching his comparison groups on potentially relevant subject factors other than carpenteredness.

Subsequent research revealed that a characteristic other than culture, environment, age, sex, or perceptual development is also important. Pollack and his associates (Pollack and Silvar, 1967; Pollack, 1970) showed that density of pigmentation in the eye is negatively related to susceptibility to the Muller-Lyer illusion. Since dark-skinned people have denser eye pigmentation, this factor offered an alternative explanation for differences between European and non-European groups in reaction to the illusion.[3] Moreover, even Berry's carefully matched Eskimo groups had differed in degree of skin pigmentation; the subjects from the more carpentered environment had somewhat lighter skin. These developments led Berry to analyze additional cross-cultural data on the illusion. He examined illusion performance in both an urban-transitional and a rural-traditional group within each of five cultures. These ten groups were ranked in terms of skin pigmentation and carpenteredness of environment. When he examined these variables as predictors of Muller-Lyer susceptibility, Berry found that skin pigmentation was the more strongly related to illusion performance. With the effect of carpenteredness removed statistically, there was a strong relationship between pigmentation and Muller-Lyer performance (Kendall's $\tau = .70$), while with the effect of pigmentation partialed out, carpenteredness was only modestly related to illusion susceptibility (Kendall's $\tau = .26$). The important point here is that Berry's first painstaking effort to provide a valid test of the carpenteredness hypothesis by matching groups on characteristics that were known to be possible artifactual sources of group differences was insufficient. A variable no one had even considered turned out to be critical, and in light of its importance the earlier research is ambiguous. There may always be (and usually *will* be) unknown factors varying between groups and impinging on the observed phenomena. Hence, matching simply cannot insure equivalence of groups as random assignment does.

In addition, matching procedures can produce their own problems. Matching is usually an expensive process, and if we match on variables unrelated to the phenomenon under study we have wasted time and effort. In addition, the systematic matching of groups on some characteristics can produce systematic "mismatching" on others. For example, in a study comparing young adults of a European country with Americans, if we match our samples on the number of years of formal schooling, we may find that the Europeans are drawn from a more highly selected and relatively advantaged group than the Americans because of the more restricted access to higher education in European countries.

Another type of matching involves equating comparison groups on some ability measure believed to be closely related to the behavior under study. (IQ is a favorite candidate in many applied settings.) This has been done frequently in cases where the effectiveness of some instruction or intervention for two groups is going to be compared. Such a procedure is not generally recommended because it frequently produces spurious effects related to statistical regression. (The appendix presents a discussion of these effects and how they can lead to faulty inferences about group differences.)

Equivalence of Treatment for Different Groups

The other main problem in comparative research is the requirement that comparison groups be provided with equivalent treatment conditions. Simply following the same procedure or using the same instructions and materials with two groups does not automatically constitute equivalent treatment. The problem exists in both general and specific forms. In general, there is reason to suspect that most standard experimental procedures are neither equally motivating for, nor equally well understood by, college students, preschoolers, retarded adolescents, schizophrenics, and Australian tribesmen. The same principle applies more specifically when the equivalence of some particular set of task materials or procedures is assessed. Every aspect of an experimenter's method — the materials, instructions, and procedure — can be a source of treatment inequivalence for different comparison groups.

Materials

In the case of task materials, the fact that the same materials are not equally familiar or meaningful to two groups is obvious when making comparisons across species or across language groups. (For example, an item in a recall task for the Kpelle of Liberia would have to be "eddoes" and not "potatoes.") But the distinction is frequently overlooked when comparing different age, education, or ethnic groups within a culture. Moreover, the requirement is not just for *some* meaningfulness and familiarity of the materials for all groups tested, but for *equality* in terms of familiarity, meaningfulness, and any other stimulus characteristic relevant to performance. In many cases the need for equal familiarity (admittedly a difficult one to satisfy) has been overlooked, and experimenters have settled for demonstrating some familiarity on the part of their potentially less proficient group — for example, by showing that the youngest subjects in a developmental study can name the objects used in the task. Such a procedure, however, is not sufficient to ensure equivalence of treatment.

Our concern with degree of familiarity and meaningfulness

should not be dismissed as quibbling. The major role that differential material meaningfulness for two groups may play in group performance differences can be illustrated by several recall studies. Typically, older subjects in a free recall task will recall more words than younger ones. While this finding has been interpreted as evidence that age groups differ in the processes they apply to the task, acceptance of such interpretations must be tempered by the fact that a given set of words is rarely as familiar or meaningful to young children as to older children or adults. And since such factors as word meaningfulness and familiarity influence the level of recall displayed by adult learners, they can also be expected to play a role in developmental differences in recall proficiency. Chi (1978) has demonstrated the importance of such familiarity factors in a study conducted with a group of children who were expert chess players and a group of graduate research assistants who were less accomplished at the game. The older subjects enjoyed the usual adult advantage over the children when recall for digits was tested, but the young chess masters outshone the adults when the items to be recalled were chess positions. The adults all had some familiarity with the recall "items" (they could all play chess), but they had less familiarity than the children. (Children are placed in this position with most recall tasks.)

In another study, Richman, Nida, and Pittman (1976) attempted to see whether recall performance would be equivalent for children of different ages if the recall items were equally familiar to younger and older subjects. These researchers developed meaningfulness ratings for different age groups on a set of three-letter words by having children say all the other words that each word from the set made them think of. Meaningfulness was defined as the average number of words thought of for the target word. As one would expect, for any given word the average meaningfulness value increased with age. When word lists were developed from these ratings such that the list administered to younger children was as meaningful for them as the older children's list was for them, there was no difference in recall performance among age groups differing by as much as four years. This lack of group performance differences stood in contrast to the case where the same list was given to two age groups; in that event, the older group, for whom the words were more meaningful, displayed better recall.

Differences in the rated quality of task materials for different groups may affect not only *quantitative* aspects of performance (as in the studies just described) but *qualitative* aspects as well. A word association study by Stolz and Tiffany (1972) illustrates this situation. In a word association task, the subject is given a series of words and asked to respond to each with the first word that comes to mind. Age groups have been shown to differ in the types of associates they produce. Adults typically give associates that are synonyms, antonyms, or superordinates of the target word and that are the same part of speech (for example, dark-light), while children's associates tend to be a different part of speech — a word that sounds like the stimulus word or one that might follow it in a sentence (dark-night). These results are often cited as corroboration for the supposition that children and adults are fundamentally different in the way they organize information. What the work of Stolz and Tiffany demonstrates, however, is that comparisons of word associations across age groups may be misleading in view of the fact that adults are much more familiar with the stimulus words than are children. These researchers constructed two lists for a word association task: the first contained adjectives that are frequently used in the English language and the second contained less commonly used synonyms for those adjectives. The first list, for example, included the words "many," "stubborn," and "neat," and the second contained "myriad," "recalcitrant," and "fastidious." College students were tested for their responses to one of the two sets of words, and afterwards their familiarity with the infrequent words was assessed in a vocabulary test. The nature of their responses varied according to which list they had received. The usual "mature" types of word associations predominated for familiar, frequent words, while "childlike" associates were typically given in response to words that were less common and familiar. The importance of the content of an experimental task is neatly demonstrated here. If the degree of familiarity and frequency of the task words affects the "maturity" of word associations provided by college students, we can make few inferences from differences observed between the word associations of different age groups when the words involved are not equally familiar to both younger and older subjects. Because the same set of words will not be equally familiar to both groups, an unbiased comparison of word association tendencies with equivalent stimuli is not easily attained.

And of course, this problem of nonequivalent task materials is not limited to studies involving verbal items. An investigation of children's concept learning by Cole (1976) illustrates the kinds of effects that theoretically irrelevant aspects of nonverbal task materials may have. In a standard concept learning task, the subject is given a series of trials on each of which he sees two stimuli varying along a number of different dimensions (such as size, shape, and color). One of the stimuli in each pair is "correct" in that it embodies the particular value of the particular dimension selected by the experimenter (for example, it is "black"). After learning to choose consistently the correct stimulus on each trial, subjects are often tested on a transfer or "shift" problem where either a different value of the same dimension (such as "white") or a value of a different dimension (such as "large," a value of size rather than color) characterizes the correct stimuli. Such tasks have been widely used in learning research with both animals and children. Children's performance on various types of transfer tasks has been assessed and interpreted as indicating whether they learn "conceptually" (respond on the basis of the relevant dimension and value), as adults do, or simply learn associations between particular items (such as the large white square) and reward. (See Medin, 1975, for a discussion of more complex conceptualizations of the processes involved in this kind of learning.) Typically, preschool children have been characterized as learning such tasks in a nonconceptual manner while older children solve the problems conceptually (Kendler and Kendler, 1962; Tighe and Tighe, 1972). Cole tested three- and five-year-olds in a concept learning study and happened to use two different sets of stimuli. One set consisted of geometric blocks similar to the materials used in most research on the topic. The other set consisted of dolls, varying in size, sex, and color. Unexpectedly, the way in which the three-year-olds performed on the transfer problems depended on which type of materials they were given. When tested with geometric blocks, fewer three-year-olds than five-year-olds were classified as conceptual learners. When tested with dolls, on the other hand, more three-year-olds performed conceptually, and there was no difference between the numbers of conceptual learners in the two age groups. Hence, whether or not age differences are found on a task that is in widespread use as an indicator of a fundamental developmental shift in learning processes appears to depend on the particular set of materials employed.

The problem of nonequivalent task materials has also affected inferences about social-class and ethnic-group differences in cognitive development. Simmons (1979) found an effect of what he calls the *cultural salience* of test materials on the sophistication of children's classification strategies. Culturally salient pictures are those showing objects, people, or activities that are both familiar and highly valued within a particular subcultural group. Previous work (Sigel, Anderson, and Shapiro, 1966; Sigel and McBane, 1967; Sigel and Olmstead, 1970) had demonstrated that children from lower-class backgrounds made less use of descriptive and categorical groupings than middle-class children when classifying pictures in the Sigel Conceptual Styles Test (SCST). Instead, the lower-class children made greater use of relational categories. Sigel (1970) suggested that such differences in categorization style reflect social-class differences in representational competence, arising because fewer "distancing experiences" (activities that heighten differentiation and abstraction) are available to children in lower-class homes. Sigel had no direct evidence for such differences in home activities; rather, he used test performance to suggest this hypothesis. Simmons (1979) felt that differences in the cultural salience of the test items for lower- and middle-class children might provide an alternative explanation for these social-class differences in picture classification, and hypothesized that such differences would be minimal if the cultural salience of the pictures was equated for subcultural groups.

To obtain appropriate stimuli, Simmons interviewed black and white middle- and lower-class children, asking them to rate their preference for and involvement in: academic-cultural activities; games and sports; and white-collar, blue-collar, and entertainer-athlete occupations. Academic-cultural activities and white-collar occupations were found to be more salient for white and middle-class children, while games and sports activities and blue-collar and entertainer-athlete occupations were more salient for black and lower-class children. Pilot testing indicated that the pictures on the SCST were, in general, culturally salient for white and middle-class children.

Simmons then constructed an eighteen-item test composed of three subsets: six of the items were selected to be culturally salient for white and middle-class children (for instance, a commercial jetliner); six were selected to be culturally salient for black and lower-class children (a professional boxer); and the last six items were selected to be neutral — that is, not differentially salient for any group of subjects (an old man playing a fiddle). For each item, children selected two pictures of the three presented that "belonged together" and gave reasons for their selections. Children were encouraged to put together more than one combination for each item, and no time limit was imposed. Both the Simmons test and the SCST (for which the same procedure was used) were administered to all the subjects, who were fifth- and sixth-grade boys fitting four combinations of ethnicity (black and white) and social class (middle- and lower-class, as determined by parental education and occupation). Children were given credit for each picture-pairing they justified on the basis of membership in a common conceptual category (for example, "they're both games you play").

Simmons replicated Sigel's finding of a social-class difference on the SCST, but did not find the effect on the Simmons test. Instead, the Simmons test showed a significant interaction of social class and ethnicity, with black lower-class children outscoring black middle-class children and with white middle-class children outscoring white lower-class children in their mean use of categorical reasons for their classifications. White children in general gave more categorical reasons on the SCST, while black children averaged more categorical reasons overall on the Simmons test. An analysis of the subsets of items on the Simmons test also showed a pattern in which subjects gave more categorical reasons for classifying items that were more salient to their subcultural group. Children of all four groups performed similarly on the "neutral" items.

Simmons' findings support his hypothesis that previous results showing social-class differences in picture classification may have been dependent upon subject-stimulus relations rather than on general conceptual styles of children from different social backgrounds. They also suggest that equating stimuli for familiarity does not go far enough in producing equivalent stimuli for some kinds of comparisons but that subjects' preferences should be considered as well.

Instructions

Instructions are another important aspect of the task for which identity does not guarantee equivalence. Clearly, we would not expect that instructions to "select the geometric pattern that correctly completes the matrix" would convey the same meaning to a college student and a four-year-old. Although this particular example is far-fetched, essentially the same situation in less blatant form appears repeatedly in the literature. Developmental psychologists frequently use the same set of task instructions with children of different ages and simply assume that those instructions will serve the same purpose for all their subjects. The vulnerability of this assumption is highlighted by a study conducted by Abramyan (1977). Her research involved a concept learning task that was somewhat different from that used by most American researchers. The stimuli were slides showing a geometric figure of a particular color against a background of a contrasting color (for example, a green circle on a yellow background). Children were told to respond to the *background* of the slide, that is, to press a button when they saw that the slide had a yellow background, but not to press it when the background was white. The children were given numerous trials on the same two slides with reinforcing instructions ("See, here it's yellow, press"). They were then given trials on a new pair of slides on which the geometric figure that had been paired with the "positive" background color was paired with the "negative" background (for instance, the negative slide might show the green circle on the white background). This shift in stimuli revealed that three-year-olds were not using the instructions to guide their performance. Instead of using the background color as the basis for their responses, they were responding on the basis of the figure that appeared on the slide. With the new slides, they incorrectly responded to the slide with the geometric figure that had been on the positive slide previously. Six-year-olds, on the other hand, responded, as instructed, on the basis of the slide background. Abramyan went on to demonstrate how the task instructions might be modified to make them equally effective for the younger children. The geometric figures were replaced with airplane silhouettes, the backgrounds were described in terms of weather conditions, and the child's task was explained as letting the plane fly (push the button) on a sunny day (yellow background) but not on a stormy day (gray background). When the task instructions were made more meaningful and salient in this fashion, three-year-olds responded on the basis of the slide backgrounds even when the airplane colors were switched.

Instructions may be inequivalent for two groups not only because groups differ in the way they understand the requirements of the task but also because groups vary in the extent to which a given set of instructions motivates or signals the need for serious effort. Goodnow (1976) has noted the prevalence of this problem in cross-cultural research. Children from non-Western cultures tend to show more improvement on an experimental task when given a second trial and told to "try hard this time" than do their Western counterparts. Goodnow comments on this effect: "It is as if, among well-socialized children in our society such phrases as 'this is a test' or 'I have some games for you to play' are sufficient cues to alert the receiver that a certain amount of effort should now be displayed. One should 'do one's best' on such occasions or, ideally, at all times" (p. 180).

Procedure

Just as an experimenter's materials often are differentially familiar for various comparison groups, so too are the activities subjects are asked to perform. Researchers ask different groups to engage in some activity that is more familiar to one group than to the other and then use differences in performance as a basis for making inferences about cognitive processes or abilities. Robert Serpell's cross-cultural work on pattern reproduction in English and Zambian school children demonstrates the fallacy inherent in this type of procedure. Previous work had shown that African and Western subjects performed similarly when asked to discriminate or react verbally to differences in stimulus orientation (Serpell, 1971a, 1971b). However, when the task included copying a stimulus *pattern*, striking differences were found between Zambian and Western children of similar educational levels (Serpell and Deregowski, 1972; Deregowski, 1972). Although other cross-cultural investigators had reported the same differences, Serpell found the contradictory results puzzling. He became concerned that these results might be restricted to a particular medium of representation employed in Western-style schools — in this case, copying figures with pencil and paper. He reasoned that the skill with which children reproduce patterns would be related to their experience in working in the particular medium selected. Accordingly, he administered three different reproduction tasks to groups of English and Zambian school children. One of the tasks, reproducing figures with modeling clay, was chosen because children from both cultures were experienced in playing with this material. A second task, reproducing patterns with wire, was selected because Zambian children have extensive experience in making wire models. The third task, copying figures with paper and pencil, was one in which English children had more practice. The children reproduced such figures as a square with diagonals, a five-pointed star, and the outline of a person. The results showed that Zambian children were more proficient than English children in reproducing the patterns in wire, while the English children made better copies with paper and pencil. The two groups performed equally well on the clay modeling task. By using several versions of the same task, Serpell was able to untangle some of the confusion caused by the subjects' seeming inability to apply processes that they seemed to use in one experimental situation (detection of differences) to a different task (reproduction) in which the investigator expected the same processes to come into play.

Seemingly minor aspects of an experimental procedure are frequently a source of treatment inequivalence. Because subjects from different groups enter an experiment with quite different experiences, knowledge, and understanding, they may be affected quite differently by some detail of the experimental procedure that is theoretically irrelevant to the cognitive skill or ability presumably being assessed. The way such details of the procedure may affect the performance of certain subject groups can be illustrated with some of the research on number conservation. In the standard number conservation task, the child is shown two parallel rows composed of equal numbers of disks and asked to judge their relative number twice. First, the child is asked whether the two rows contain the same number of disks when they are aligned in one-to-one correspondence (producing rows of equal lengths), and then he is questioned a second time after one of the rows has been rearranged—either spread out or made more compact so that the two rows are no longer equal in length. Typically, young children say that the two rows no longer contain the same number of disks after one row has been rearranged, while older children continue to judge the two rows as equal in number. Rose and Blank (1974) have argued that certain details of this procedure may be involved in the young child's apparent failure to understand that rearranging items does not change their number. Because in everyday situations the child would not be asked the same question about number a second time unless some significant change had occurred, the standard testing procedure suggests that a different answer is now appropriate. Rose and Blank demonstrated that if the task is modified so that the child is asked to overtly compare the rows only once, after the rearrangement, first graders are much better at giving conserving responses.

McGarrigle and Donaldson (1974-75) developed a similar idea. They based their argument on the general notion that the young child who is still in the process of mastering language depends on the nonlinguistic aspects of a social interaction to provide a context for deriving meaning from speech. In the conservation of number task, as described above, the second judgment about relative number is asked for immediately after the experimenter has rearranged one row of disks. While a question about number would normally be considered irrelevant in the context of this transformation, a question about length would be highly relevant. If the young child relies more on the experimenter's actions than on her words to interpret what is being asked, the child will conclude that the more logical question about length is at issue here, and in answering the length question will fail in the standard task. McGarrigle and Donaldson found support for this notion by investigating what happened if the rearrangement of the row appeared to be the result of an accident rather than of deliberate action by the experimenter. They found a powerful effect for this manipulation: while only thirteen of the eighty young children they tested conserved in the standard version of the task, where the transformation appeared intentional, fifty conserved after an "accidental" transformation. Thus, whether or not an experimenter obtains a difference between younger and older children in terms of number conservation (and thus what inferences she draws concerning cognitive differences associated with age) may depend upon such theoretically irrelevant details of the testing procedure as whether she asks for number judgments once or twice and whether the row rearrangement appears accidental or intentional.

Blank and Rose (1975) demonstrated that differences in methodology *within a study* can lead to misinterpretation of patterns of results. They were concerned with an inconsistency found in previous research on children's cross-modal transfer of a form discrimination. In a cross-modal transfer task, the child is first presented with two forms in one modality (say, visually) until he has learned to consistently choose the form designated as correct. Then the same two forms are presented in another modality (for example, tactually, by allowing the child to feel the two forms but not to see them) to ascertain whether the child will pick the same form that he had learned to choose in the other modality (shows a transfer effect). In an earlier study, Blank, Altman, and Bridger (1968) found that preschoolers would transfer a discrimination they had learned in the visual modality to the tactual modality but would not transfer a discrimination learned tactually to the visual modality. The results suggested that preschoolers do not have an efficient means for encoding tactual information. However, Blank and her colleagues suspected that the asymmetry between children's visual-to-tactual and tactual-to-visual cross-modal transfer resulted, in part, from differences in test methods used in the two modalities. The visual task required the subject to lift the stimulus he thought was correct from a platform and pick up a reward from underneath if the choice was the right one. In the tactual version, the stimuli were placed in the child's hands; he was asked to relinquish the one he thought to be correct, and was handed a reward if he made the right choice. One of these procedures might have been more difficult for the child to perform, regardless of modality.

To test for this possibility, Blank and Rose first measured how long preschool children take to learn the identical form discrimination in each modality (visual and tactual) and presentation condition (platform and hand-held). They found that when children held the stimuli (which, in the visual condition, were encased in clear plastic boxes so that the children could not feel the shapes), they learned more rapidly for both the visual and tactual modalities. In a second study, children were tested for cross-modal transfer of a form discrimination; this time, however, the "hand-held" condition that had been associated with easier learning was used in the two conditions. The subjects performed equally well in visual-to-tactual and tactual-to-visual transfer once the confounding effect of differences in stimulus presentation was removed.

Interactions of task features

To complicate matters further, features of the task procedure, materials, and instructions may interact with one another and with a group's past experience and knowledge about the "rules of the experimental game" to lead one group of subjects to interpret the task in one way while another group interprets it quite differently. Blank (1975) has demonstrated this type of effect within the context of a discrimination learning task. In this task the child is shown a pair of stimuli over repeated trials and is reinforced for selecting one of them, regardless of its position in the pair. For example, a red circle may be paired with a red triangle, with the red circle always designated as correct. Young children can easily learn to make the right choice consistently, but they appear to be unable, curiously, to explain the basis for their choice. When asked "Why did you choose that picture?" they either fail to respond or give an apparently irrelevant answer, such as "Because I wanted candy," instead of giving an appropriate answer ("Because it's a circle") as older subjects do. Blank pointed out that what the experimenter is really asking with the "why" question is "What characteristic of that object led you to identify it as correct?" This conflicts with the nature of "Why did you" questions in the child's everyday experience, when such queries usually refer to the child's motivation for some action. While the older child and adult know enough about the nature of a testing situation to realize that the experimenter is not likely to be asking about their motive for deciding to choose the correct stimulus, the young child may lack this awareness.

To test her hypothesis, Blank gave a group of preschoolers a discrimination learning task and then asked them about the basis for their responses in one of several different ways. Half the children were asked either how they knew which stimulus concealed the candy or why they chose the stimulus they did. The remaining children were asked, "Which one had the candy?" Within each of these groups, half the children were questioned with the stimuli in front of them, while the other half were questioned after the stimuli were out of sight. Children questioned with the stimuli in front of them just pointed to the correct one when asked either type of question. With the stimuli out of view, almost all the children with the "which" question gave an appropriate answer, while children interrogated with the "how" or "why" question almost never did. Thus, the study demonstrates that task procedures and instructions may interact to affect the type of performance certain subject groups exhibit. "Mature" answers were given only when the task stimuli were out of sight and children were asked which item was correct rather than why they chose the one they did. In effect, the procedure is part of the instructions because the subject relies on the experimenter's actions as well as his words as a source of clues as to what the task is all about.[4] In addition, the subjects' understanding of the nature of an experiment will shape their interpretation of task demands. Age, culture, and ability groups differ in their knowledge concerning the type of answers and behavior that are appropriate in an experiment. Because these differences exist, the same set of task instructions and procedures may not be equally understandable for different groups.

Hence, we can rarely say with assurance that a certain experimental treatment is really equivalent for two comparison groups. As the examples have demonstrated, nominally identical treatments are often psychologically inequivalent. If we vary our procedures or instructions for different groups to try to achieve psychological equivalence (for example, by giving younger children a more detailed set of instructions and fewer problems to solve than older children), we are still faced with the question whether our efforts have really achieved that end. There is no straightforward standard for assessing the equivalence of treatment for two comparison groups. Setting equivalent performance as the standard for demonstrating treatment equivalence would only ensure that legitimate differences between groups could never be found. This dilemma reflects a fundamental weakness in experimental designs in which different subject groups are compared in terms of performance on a single cognitive task.

Limitations of Simple Descriptions of Group Differences

We have argued that the very nature of comparative research means that we cannot be sure we have provided equivalent treatment to both our comparison groups, and even if we assume that we have, we cannot be sure which of the many differences between our groups was responsible for any observed performance difference. The design of comparative studies simply does not justify the kinds of statements about causal relationships that are the basic goal of experimental research. One response to this design problem is to forego causal interpretations of comparative studies and treat their results as we do the finding of a correlation between two subject characteristics, that is, as an indication that two qualities tend to covary without any implication that one of them causes the other. (Wood, 1974, takes this approach.) One can argue for the usefulness of simply describing the differences in performance for different groups even if those differences cannot be causally related to any one variable. "After all," runs the argument, "it's educationally useful to know that five-year-olds have problems copying geometric shapes that eight-year-olds appear to have overcome, no matter what the reason for the difference."

There is a basic fault with this line of logic, however. If we cannot establish unambiguously what differences in cognitive processing produced the differences in performance — that is, which one of the many preexisting differences between five- and eight-year-olds is linked to the apparent differences in their figure-copying skills — any descriptive statement of results may prove highly misleading. Both theory development and the practical application of research results will be seriously handicapped if differences in cognitive functioning are attributed to the wrong subject variable. The data on group differences in susceptibility to visual illusions can serve as an illustration of the limitations on useful application, and also the wasted effort, that incomplete understanding of the sources of cognitive differences can produce. Susceptibility to the Muller-Lyer illusion was studied in over two thousand people from more than fourteen cultures scattered all around the globe before the findings of Pollack, Berry, and others demonstrated that density of eye pigmentation might be contributing to the results.

From a pragmatic viewpoint, simple descriptions of group differences in this case are insufficient because they provide little insight into the kinds of measures that would have to be taken to improve a group's cognitive performance. Relative to European or American samples, sub-Saharan Africans have been described as having particular problems with tasks that require the manipulation of spatial relations or detection of contours; the Muller-Lyer illusion is but one example of such a task. One practical use of this skill is in detecting the magnitude of altitude or depth changes when depicted on a map by gradations in color shade. The practitioner might decide to try to help African students by providing special training in discriminating between color chips of various shades and in detecting contours represented by variations in shading in order to further their skill in detecting depth on maps. Although somewhat premature, such an intervention program might seem reasonable in view of descriptions of the apparent deficits of African students in performing this kind of task. However, two studies in which Jahoda (1971, 1975) examined African and Scottish university students' color perception as it relates to spatial perception undermine the rationale for this kind of intervention effort. The denser eye pigmentation implicated in Africans' relatively low susceptibility to the Muller-Lyer illusion has been shown to produce also a lower sensitivity to blue light. In his first study on this problem, Jahoda found that Africans had more trouble with a map-contour-detection task when dealing with areas of water, which were portrayed in shades of blue, than when dealing with hills, which were depicted in reddish-brown shades, while the two types of problems were of equivalent difficulty for Scottish students. Hence, if the practitioner wanted to improve the map-contour-detection skills of African students, the most obvious first step would be to color the map's water areas in shades of a color more readily detected by persons with densely pigmented retinas. However, in his follow-up study, Jahoda (1975) allowed subjects more time to make their responses and then related their performance to a test of spatial ability. Under the revised conditions, changing the color of the contour lines did not change their performance, and no relation was obtained between sensitivity to blue contour lines and performance on the spatial ability test. The moral of the story, for our purposes, is that effective efforts toward reducing the apparent cognitive deficit of one particular group relative to another must be based on more than just a descriptive statement of observed performance differences. We have to know the exact circumstances under which the deficit will appear, what processes are involved in the task of interest, and how people differ in the way they employ those processes in different circumstances.

Relating Group Differences to Underlying Causes

In chapter 2 we emphasized that the major difficulty associated with research in cognitive psychology arises because the activities of central interest, the cognitive processes we would like to specify, are not generally accessible to direct observation. Cognitive processes (or structures, or abilities) are never measured in isolation. In fact, they are not even definable in isolation. Both the definition and measurement of cognitive activities rest upon the study of behavior in well-defined tasks where we can be pretty certain of the various stimuli that the subject is responding to and the responses that are a part of her repertoire.

The need to deal with the effects of task-specific factors in assessing some presumably general type of cognitive activity (remembering, rehearsing, associating), coupled with our often dim understanding of what these task-specific factors are, is one of the major sources of complexity in designing experiments to isolate the effects of individual variables in noncomparative cognitive psychology. Several studies are needed to choose among hypotheses, and unless the hypothesis is reasonably specific, it may be testable only within the context of a series of experiments linked by a theory.

When we move to comparative studies of the sort we have begun to discuss in this chapter, the inferential difficulties we face are extremely serious. None of the all-other-things-equal assumptions that we could use to avoid a lot of work in noncomparative research is available to us. We cannot assume that all subjects understand instructions in the same way; we cannot assume that the stimuli within the experiment proper are equivalent for all of them (that is, equally familiar, equally easy to tell apart, or equally associated with one another). Most important, we cannot assign our subjects at random to the relevant experimental conditions and then assume that these kinds of nonequivalences apply equally to all groups.

In short, we are in trouble. Our task would be simplified if we were willing to stop short and simply demonstrate a group difference in a specified task. But long lists of similarities and differences between a group of interest and some comparison group do not yield much leverage for understanding the sources of the differences or for helping to design programs of treatment in the many cases where providing treatment is the ultimate goal of the research.

There is, in our view, no easy road of escape from this trouble. It is part of the logic of the enterprise. There are, however, a variety of strategies that can be employed to reduce the risk of inferential nonsense. Before considering these in detail in chapters 4 and 5, we will illustrate how the difficulties we have been discussing can weaken a piece of research by describing a published comparative study. Since research in this domain is easily criticized for its weaknesses and our concern is to illustrate the *general* classes of errors that comparative cognitive research generates, we will leave out enough detail to render the study anonymous. However, the rationale, methods, and results described below are real; they were taken from the published report.

The study in question was based on the general hypothesis that free recall clustering is a measure of the organizational processes that underlie not only verbal recall but also such skills as reading comprehension. In this particular case, a lack of organizational processing was hypothesized to characterize mentally retarded individuals and was considered a possible source of their problems in understanding what they read. To investigate this hypothesis, a population of mentally retarded adolescents was obtained and a standardized reading test administered. On the basis of scores on this test, the sample was divided into two groups, one scoring above and one below the sample median in reading comprehension. These two groups of subjects were then given four recall trials on a single list containing five items from each of four categories. Since the researchers' ultimate goal was to improve reading comprehension by training retardates to organize verbal material, the list was presented in two ways. For half the subjects in each group, the category instances were randomly ordered on all four trials. For the other subjects, the words were blocked (category instances presented sequentially) on the first two trials and randomly ordered on the second two trials. The major results were that above-average readers clustered more than below-average readers, and that subjects who were given blocked category instances on the first two trials displayed more clustering than those with random presentation on the final two (random-order) trials as well as on the first two (blocked) trials. From these results, the following conclusions were drawn: the hypothesis about a relationship between clustering and reading comprehension is correct; it is possible to increase organization in recall; and it might be possible, by remediating deficiencies in retarded subjects' input organization of verbal materials, to facilitate reading comprehension.

Let us examine this study in terms of the problems that typify comparative cognitive research. Although an attempt has been made to relate a difference between two groups in task performance (in reading, or actually, in reading and clustering) to some more basic and general cognitive process (the organization of verbal information), the exact nature of this process as applied to reading comprehension is not specified. In addition, ambiguity arises because the nature of the processes involved in clustering is the subject of sharp debate, as is the assumption that clustering is a direct cause of remembering. In other words, we find neither analyses of the recall and of the comprehension task and the role that organization plays within each nor a direct measure of the "organizational skill" that is presumed to underlie group performance differences. In the absence of some direct measure of organizational processes, a relationship between reading comprehension and clustering performance, as obtained here, could reflect *any* common process that we might care to hypothesize (such as verbal ability of some sort, motivation, or attention). As we have already argued, this problem in trying to draw process inferences from task performance differences is rampant within comparative cognitive research. If we were comparing different treatment groups rather than different subject groups, we might at least be able to attribute the performance difference to a given independent variable, even if the cognitive process that was involved remained elusive. In the comparative case, even that help is denied us.

The significance of a difference between the random and blocked presentation conditions is likewise difficult to interpret without an explicit model of task performance. Just what is being trained during the blocked presentation — that is, what it is that subjects with blocked lists are doing differently from subjects with random lists — has not been specified. The claim that the study demonstrates the possibility of increasing retardates' clustering during recall is especially weak because the design does not permit us to disentangle categorical clustering from rote learning. When category instances are presented in blocked format on the study trial, category members may be recalled successively not because subjects are using categories to organize their recall but just because they are recalling items according to their input order. A difference in clustering scores between blocked and randomly presented lists is therefore not impressive. Although the group with blocked presentation on the first two trials also showed more clustering on the third and fourth trials (when their study list was no longer blocked), these scores could simply reflect the influence of rote learning on previous trials with the same list.[5]

In addition to failing to present a convincing process interpretation of the findings (and this difficulty is also common in noncomparative cognitive psychology), the study suffers from the sorts of threats to internal validity that are endemic to comparative research. The researchers intended to use an existing group difference in reading skill to test a hypothesis about the role of organizational processes in reading and clustering. The basic problem of obtaining comparable groups when testing for the effect of a particular subject variable is clearly present here. Although the subjects used in this study were all labeled as "mentally retarded adolescents," there was probably considerable variation among the subjects in terms of IQ and chronological age (the categories "retarded" and "adolescent" both cover a great deal of territory) and in terms of other relevant factors such as length of institutionalization, prior exposure to academic testing, and level of motivation. When the sample was divided into two subgroups on the basis of reading scores, the subgroups almost certainly differed in terms of these other variables as well. What is described in the study as a relationship between clustering and reading comprehension could really be a relationship between clustering and IQ, chronological age, motivation level, or any other characteristic that might vary between the two "reading" groups.

The assumption of equivalence of treatment for the groups must also be considered suspect. Although the words on the free recall list were presented in both the visual and the auditory modes, a difference in reading ability may have meant that it was harder for the poorer readers to comprehend the input, a necessary step before they could learn it. Moreover, auditory-phonological impairment could well be one cause for the poorer readers' comprehension deficiencies, and such a difference could make auditory as well as visual perception of the items more difficult for them.

Limiting our conclusions regarding the subject difference to a description of the effect (such as "retarded subjects with relatively high reading comprehension scores cluster more during free recall than those with relatively low reading comprehension scores") would not solve our problem. First, in light of the many other differences that could characterize the two reading groups, the statement may be highly misleading. Second, a simple statement of performance differences is an inadequate basis for drawing inferences about educational remediation, the goal that motivated the study. Such prescriptions must be based on a causal explanation of the deficit. If it is not a difference in the use of organizational processes that *causes* the difference in reading comprehension, there is no point in trying to teach organizational skills in order to improve reading.

4.

Comparing Tasks and Groups

The simplest approach to comparative cognitive research entails selecting a task presumed to measure some cognitive process or ability; administering the task to two groups of subjects varying in sex, marital status, social class, culture, age, or some other characteristic; and then reporting which group demonstrates more of the ability or process under study. The major threats to validity that weaken this approach were discussed in chapter 3. Primarily, there are two problems: we cannot ensure that our experimental treatment is really equivalent for the two groups; and, even if it is (and the differences observed are legitimate in this regard), we have no way of pinpointing the cause of these differences in terms of specific cognitive processes.

This chapter and the next present a number of research strategies that have been developed to cope with these difficulties. The strategies described in this chapter all involve instituting variations in a cognitive task and assessing the impact of those variations on different subject groups. The next chapter discusses various model-based approaches in which the researcher develops several models of cognitive performance representing different strategies or knowledge levels and tries to devise the task in such a way that a subject's behavior will reveal which model, if any, corresponds to his processes in pursuing the task.

Our classification of the various research approaches into different strategies should not be taken too strictly. We have tried to provide an organization for these methods that captures their essential differences, but they are all really variations on a single theme. They all depend upon breaking down the task being studied into component subtasks that implicate discrete cognitive processes, and they all attempt to relate performance within groups and between groups to the underlying processes indexed by the subtasks.

Careful analysis of the tasks that we use to "diagnose" thinking is central to all cognitive psychological research, but its centrality to comparative cognitive research needs to be emphasized. Too often the tasks used in comparative studies assume that a strong relationship exists between those tasks and the underlying cognitive processes of interest. This assumption is not acceptable in noncomparative research, and if anything, there is even less reason to accept it when we begin to use standard cognitive tasks in a program of comparative research.

Because the cognitive tasks do not provide straightforward measures of individual processes, we cannot simply compare performance levels for two subject groups and then assert that one group has more of some process than another, or worse yet, that it has a monopoly on the process. In order to relate group differences in cognition to specific processes, we have to analyze our experimental tasks thoroughly and then develop a strategy for measuring separately the particular processes employed by our two subject groups (either directly or by assessing the impact various manipulations have on performance). This undertaking amounts to the union of the "theory of the task" and the "theory of the subject" referred to earlier. The research strategies described in this chapter and the next provide some examples of what forms such a union might take.

The sample comparative study on reading comprehension and recall clustering that was described at the end of the last chapter illustrates the interpretive problem posed by using tasks that have not been carefully analyzed. Even in noncomparative research, when we are fairly confident about what independent variable (in operational terms) produces the performance difference, our hypotheses about the internal mental processes to which the variable is linked are often controversial and indeed faulty. In comparative studies cognitive processes are even harder to track down because we really do not know what independent variable is being "manipulated." (This was the case in the research on rigidity with retardates in which Zigler tried to show that the relevant operational variable was not IQ but the amount of previous social contact.) In addition, while noncomparative research generally tries to demonstrate that a certain process plays *some* role in task performance, comparative research attempts to quantify the extent of that role in order to compare its magnitudes in different subject groups. This latter undertaking is considerably more difficult: it requires a more careful analysis of the task and of the way the different processes interact as the task is performed.

A specific example will clarify this argument about the added importance of task analysis in comparative research. False-recognition tasks are a currently popular method for studying developmental differences in the way items are stored in memory. Researchers in this area make the theoretical assumption that words are encoded in memory not as intact units but as bundles of features or attributes. The way a word sounds, what it looks like in print, the various aspects of its meaning, and the other words associated with it are all candidates for the attributes that people might store in memory (Underwood, 1969). The false-recognition paradigm has been developed as a means for investigating the particular types of features most involved in recognition memory. In one of these tasks, a subject is given a long list of words, some of which are repeated. As each item is presented, the subject has to indicate whether it is a "new" one (previously unseen) or an "old" one (a word that has appeared previously). The experimenter places a number of distractor items on the list — words that have not appeared before but that partially resemble previous words in terms of some attribute, such as sound; for example, the word "hat" may appear on the list and be followed by "cat" some thirty words later. If subjects tend to recognize falsely a particular type of distractor (such as rhymes of previous words) more than they do miscellaneous new words, the experimenter concludes that the relevant feature (in this case, sound) plays a role in recognition memory.

So far there has been no real analysis of the way in which subjects make their recognition decisions in this task. When a single subject population is tested and the only question is whether a particular attribute plays *some* role in recognition, the false-recognition technique appears reasonable, but the failure to analyze the task becomes more troublesome when the technique is employed in comparative studies. The false-recognition task has been used in many comparative studies to uncover developmental differences in the features that are encoded in memory (Bach and Underwood, 1970; Felzen and Anisfeld, 1970; Freund and Johnson, 1972; Hall and Halperin, 1972; Cramer, 1973). In these developmental studies, researchers were comparing the number of false recognitions for each distractor type across age groups (for example, seeing if fifth graders were more or less likely than second graders to falsely recognize rhymes) and concluding on this basis that the corresponding attribute was more (or less) important in memory at one age than at another. In the context of noncomparative research conducted with adults, this strategy may at first appear to be a logical way to proceed. However, even the most rudimentary attempt to analyze the false-recognition task reveals that quantitative comparisons resting on differences in false-recognition rates are basically unsound. On the recognition test the subject presumably encodes each word in terms of some set of features and then compares the set to those she has encoded for previous list words. The more closely the attributes of the present item match those of a previous item, the more likely the subject is to judge the present item as "old." If a distractor resembles an old item in terms of sound but the subject does not do any encoding of the acoustic properties of list items, she is unlikely to recognize falsely a lot of rhyme distractors (for example, to think a word like "cat" is old after she has been given "hat"). However, if the subject not only encodes sound features but does so with great accuracy, she will react in the same way—she will assert that "cat" is a new word because although it sounds similar to "hat" it doesn't sound the same. Thus while the false-recognition paradigm may be useful in showing that a certain type of feature plays *some* role in item recognition, it does not work well in making quantitative comparisons concerning the *size* of that role for different subject groups.[1] When older children are found to make fewer false recognitions of rhymes than younger children, it is not clear whether the effect indicates *less* or *better* encoding of acoustic features at the older age.

Although it is unlikely that a seat-of-the-pants analysis of the recognition task such as this could provide a complete or totally accurate model of word recognition, almost any such analysis would suggest that differences between groups in false-recognition rates would be uninterpretable. Means and Rohwer (1976) attempted to increase the interpretability of the task by using labeled pictures as list items so that the distractor would be identical to previous items in terms of the attribute of interest though still distinguishable on the basis of other types of features (for instance, a piece of archery equipment and a ribbon, both labeled "bow"). Although this modification of the task reduced one source of ambiguity in the data, it is apparent that the task was still insufficiently analyzed. Other aspects of task performance—the overall level of difficulty, the tendency to guess "old" under a given degree of uncertainty, the awareness that the list contained distractor items—are likely to differ for different subject groups and to interact with the subjects' patterns of attribute encoding. Without a more detailed analysis of the task and the behaviors it elicits we cannot modify it to separate out the effects of possible changes in the types of features that children encode.

Relating overt performance differences to specific cognitive processes, never an easy undertaking, is particularly difficult when conducting comparative research. Task analysis is hardly an easy solution to the problem, but it does reveal where important ambiguities exist and can save researchers the time and effort that would otherwise be wasted in conducting experiments that could only yield uninterpretable data. In the comparative case, in fact, we see little hope of relating group differences to processing differences without using a task analysis, developed and tested in a series of interlocking studies. All of the comparative research strategies to be described in this chapter and the next involve some sort of analysis of the task under study. Sometimes the analysis is more or less implicit, as in the strategies described in this chapter; sometimes the analysis is explicit, as in the different versions of the model-based approach discussed in the next chapter.

Comparing Patterns of Performance

While it is essential to recognize the importance of working with tasks for which we have a theory relating performance to underlying process, it is unreasonable to expect researchers to wait for *the* correct analysis of some set of cognitive tasks before employing those tasks in a comparative framework. Such a course of action would not only be unreasonably conservative, but it would also be misguided, for it would assume that this "correct analysis" exists and is an entity independent of the subjects and of the circumstances surrounding the nominal tasks. In practice, it is often because researchers wish to obtain more information about how a task is dealt with that they introduce it to a new population of subjects, hoping that these subjects will help to reveal, by the way they work on the task, hitherto unnoticed components.

Accepting the inevitability that difficulties will arise because our theories of cognitive activity in specialized task environments are incomplete (if not outright mistaken), we need to go about the comparative research enterprise in ways that will minimize the threats to valid inference from our observations. The approaches we find most useful are those that subordinate direct comparisons *between* group performances to an analysis of the patterns of performance *within* the groups being compared. Once the patterns of performance on two or more cognitive tasks or on two or more aspects of the same task have been examined, the similarity or dissimilarity of these patterns may be compared across groups.

An illustration of the purest form of this strategy — making qualitative comparisons of performance patterns — is provided by Rosch's (1977) research on the nature of color categories and their relationship to other cognitive processes such as memory.

For some time anthropologists and psychologists have been interested in the notion that a people's language affects the nature of their understanding of the world. As formulated by Whorf (1956), the influence of language on understanding begins with our perceptual system; language shapes the basic information we extract from our environment. Because color is a stimulus dimension that can be objectively quantified in terms of wavelength and is a part of everyone's experience (except for those who are color blind), it has become a popular domain for the study of this linguistic relativity hypothesis. Brown and Lenneberg (1954) conducted a study in which they showed that a highly codable color (a color that is labeled quickly, with a short name, and with the same name by most people) is later recognized more readily than other colors. The implication of this phenomenon was that since different languages divide up the color space differently (have different color terms), the colors that speakers of different languages would tend to remember best would differ in wavelength but would be constant in terms of codability.

Berlin and Kay (1969) challenged the notion that different language groups perceive colors differently. They demonstrated that if speakers from many different language groups are given a wide variety of color chips and asked for the best examples of their color categories, they will all tend to select the same chips. Although the number of color categories varies among language groups, there is an upper limit of eleven on the number of categories used, and the best examples of the categories used in different groups tend to be the same. The inference suggested by these results is that these "best examples," called focal colors, have a physiological basis that renders them perceptually salient for humans. Rosch hypothesized that it was the fact that these colors are the most typical examples of their color categories, not that they are easily labeled, that made them more recognizable in Brown and Lenneberg's study. She tested her hypothesis by finding a group of subjects among whom the vocabulary used to describe colors made it possible to separate focality from codability. She chose the Dani of New Guinea, who have only two basic color terms, and set out to determine if the relationship between focality and memory for colors would hold up in a group for whom focal colors are not more codable.

It was crucial to the logic of Rosch's study that she did not ask the question "Do the Dani remember focal colors as well as Americans do?" Instead, the patterns of responding within Dani culture and within her American group most interested her. The question she addressed was whether the pattern of re-membering focal and nonfocal colors is the same for Dani and Americans. This point is important because a host of factors could influence the level of recall in each of the groups Rosch worked with. But if her analysis was correct, the pattern of responding within cultures should remain invariant across cultures, even if one group remembered colors better in overall terms.

Following the procedures used by Brown and Lenneberg, Rosch conducted a pilot study in which she elicited names for each item of a large set of color chips. She reported that focal colors and nonfocal colors are not differentially codable among the Dani, as they are among Americans. Then the subjects were shown one color chip at a time, and after a delay of thirty seconds they were asked to pick that target color chip from an array containing many colors. True to her hypothesis, the focal colors were easier to recognize than the nonfocal colors in both the Dani and American groups (Heider, 1972).[2]

The strategy of comparing patterns rather than levels of per-formance for different groups is essentially a conservative one. The conceptual difficulties inherent in comparative research are taken most seriously by researchers using this approach. The underlying reasoning is that there are so many potential sources for any group differences in performance that compar-ing the proficiency levels of two groups or even the magnitude of some effect (such as the difference between recognition levels for focal and nonfocal colors) is of very limited utility. But not all approaches to the study of comparative cognition require giving up the comparison of group performance levels.

The Group by Task Interaction Approach

The second research strategy is somewhat less conservative because it takes into account direct comparisons between groups as well as differences in patterns of responding. The essence of this approach is to present each group with at least two tasks. The tasks are chosen so that if the researcher's hypothesis about the source of group differences in cognition is correct, the groups will differ on only one of the tasks. The task that is chosen to eliminate differences in performance (the control task) is made identical to the standard experimental task *except* that it does not require some single structure or process that one group is hypothesized to possess or employ to a greater degree than the other group.

Bryant (1974) has argued for the necessity of using this kind of strategy in developmental research:

> The main difficulty seems to lie in the use of age as a variable. Many psychologists have been content to find a simple age difference and to base their very specific conclusions on this one difference. This is almost always unjustified because one task will involve various aspects of behavior and the age difference could mean a change in one or more of these. Almost always one needs an added control task which is similar to the experimental task in all ways *except* the aspect under inspection. If an age difference is found in performance on the experimental task but not on the control task, the experimenter can then begin to conclude something specific about development. Experiments on specific developmental changes should look for an interaction between age and tasks (experimental *and* control) and not just an age difference in a single task.   (p.172)

When groups attain equivalent performance levels on one of the tasks in a Group × Task design, the problems of ensuring treatment equivalence and group compatibility are greatly reduced because it is then unlikely that many artifacts, such as differential motivation or familiarity with task materials, could have produced the group difference on the second task without producing a corresponding difference on the first. A cross-cultural study comparing information-processing in Kpelle tribesmen of Liberia and Americans (Cole, Gay, and Glick, 1968) illustrates the usefulness of this approach in a situation where the number of potential alternative explanations for group performance differences would have been tremendous if only a single version of the task had been given to the two groups. The experiment involved testing the accuracy of number judgments when varying numbers of dots were shown on a tachistoscope for very brief time intervals. The Kpelle and American groups differed greatly both in terms of their familiarity with such experimental tasks and in terms of the apparatus and the details of the procedure used in testing them. For example, the Kpelle were tested in the back of a dimly lit village store with music and beer-drinking going on out in front, rather than in the confines of a university laboratory; and in contrast to the sophisticated piece of equipment employed in America, the tachistoscope used with the Kpelle was jerry-built from a tin box and a set of goggles and had to be powered by batteries. Because of these differences, innumerable possible interpretations could have been given to a general finding that Americans judged the number of dots more accurately than the Kpelle. However, Cole, Gay, and Glick were able to show that the two groups performed equivalently with small numbers of dots, while the Americans were distinctly better with large numbers. Since both of these findings were obtained within the same experimental procedure and setting, arguments that the Kpelle's poorer showing with large numbers of dots was the result of theoretically irrelevant variables, such as discomfort in the testing situation, poor eyesight, lack of understanding of the task requirements, or fear of the tachistoscopic apparatus, would be unconvincing. The additional fact that the pattern of errors on large numbers of dots was the same for both groups when the dots were randomly arranged but was dissimilar with patterned arrays (in a direction indicating the Americans' greater use of pattern) again implied that the observed processing differences were genuine ones rather than artifacts of some irrelevant source of treatment inequivalence.

The interpretive power that can be gained from this approach should be clear. However, a Group × Task design cannot rule out all doubts about group or treatment inequivalences. The approach takes care of these problems only to the extent that any differences in extraneous subject variables between groups affect the two tasks equally: that is, there are no interactions between task variations and some theoretically irrelevant subject variable on which the groups differ. For example, looking at the Cole, Gay, and Glick results, one could argue that uncorrected poor eyesight would have a greater negative effect on the perception of large numbers of dots than on the perception of small numbers of dots because when varying numbers of figures are placed inside the same frame, the fewer figures there are, the more white space there will be between them. An interaction between vision impairment and the number of dots being judged, then, is a potential rival explanation of the results obtained by Cole, Gay, and Glick. Other findings obtained within this study (the fact that the Kpelle benefited as much from patterning with large numbers of dots as with small numbers) reduce the plausibility of this interpretation, but even so it does serve to illustrate the ever present logical possibility that irrelevant differences between two tasks and between two subject groups interact to produce artifactual Group × Task interactions. In addition, the more differences there are between the two tasks in the design, the more likely such troublesome interactions become.

This strategy is vulnerable also to errors of interpretation resulting from an inadequate analysis of the processes involved in the experimental and control tasks. While the Group × Task design allows us to rule out many artifactual explanations of group differences, the researcher's atrribution of a difference on one of the tasks to any particular process of theoretical interest is only as valid as his task analysis. Ideally, the two tasks used in this type of research should be well understood and isomorphic except for a single requirement. If the difference or differences between the two tasks are not known, any process inference based on the fact that the two groups differ on one task but not the other is going to be on shaky ground. Moreover, if the tasks differ in more ways than one (as most do), just looking at performance differences will fall short of the goal of isolating the source of group differences in cognitive processing.

Rohwer (1976) has offered a detailed description of the use of this type of research strategy within an instructional context. His discussion focuses on the most frequently encountered case, where one group (or individual) performs in some task in a manner viewed as less proficient than that of another. The next steps in Rohwer's approach involve hypothesizing a specific locus for the group difference and then designing a variation of the original task that will provide compensation for the perceived deficiency in the low-scoring group and thus eliminate the group difference.[3]

The basics of the approach can be illustrated with some of Rohwer's own research on developmental changes in the way people learn to associate items (paired-associate learning). In a standard paired-associate task, the subject is presented with a series of pairs of nouns and instructed to learn each pair so that when he is shown one of the items from the pair at test, he will be able to produce the other. Typically, older children are able to recall more associates than are younger children. Rohwer has hypothesized that this age difference in paired-associate learning performance is the result of a developmental difference in propensity to engage in a process termed elaboration, in which the subject invokes some unifying context for the two nouns (Rohwer, 1973). If elaboration of the presented pairs is the requirement for efficient paired-associate learning that younger children lack, a variation of the task in which that context is provided by the experimenter should improve their performance. Two prominent means of supplying an elaborative context — presenting the two nouns within a unifying sentence ("The *cow* wore the *tie*") and portraying them as interacting pictures (a drawing of a cow with a tie around its neck) — have produced dramatic facilitation in the performance of younger children relative to their performance on the standard task.

To make the Group × Task design explicit: two age groups (younger and older subjects) are tested on two versions of the paired-associate task (the standard task and the compensatory version in which elaborative sentences or pictures are provided). If the hypothesis is correct, the younger children will perform more poorly than older ones on the standard version of the task but not on the compensatory version. Figure 4.1 illustrates this type of interaction.

Of course, an experimenter's findings will not always conform to this idealized picture. Rohwer has discussed the interpretations that may be drawn from various patterns of group differences on two tasks. The hypothesis is fully confirmed only if the compensatory task provides sufficient benefit for the improficient learners to bring them up to the level of the proficient learners *and* if it does not produce any improvement in proficient learners relative to their standard task performance (as in figure 4.1). We have already shown that obtaining equivalent performances from comparison groups on one version of the task is important in order to rule out alternative accounts of group differences on the standard task in terms of treatment inequivalencies. The importance of obtaining equivalent performance on the compensatory task is stressed also in Rohwer's discussion because other outcomes are ambiguous (as well as less than fully consistent with the research hypothesis).[4] Rohwer points out that if the compensatory task is beneficial for improficient learners but does not raise their

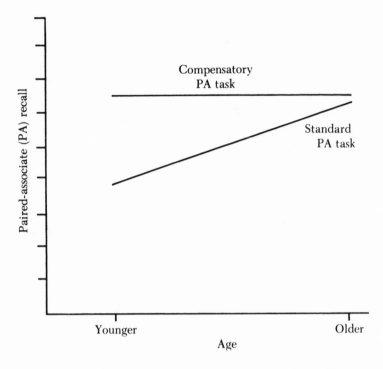

Figure 4.1. Positive test of the elaboration hypothesis in a Group × Task design. Adapted from Rohwer, 1976, p. 81, fig. 1.

performance level to that of proficient learners in the standard task, it is possible either that (1) the modification incorporated in the compensatory task is not sufficient to consistently activate the relevant process or strategy in improficient learners, or that (2) there is some additional source of group differences besides that compensated for in the modified version of the task. We would add that these potential additional sources of group differences could include not only other processes involved in the task besides that under study but also artifacts stemming from a failure to provide equivalent treatment conditions for the two groups. If the modified task facilitates performance not only in the improficient group but in proficient learners too, it may be either that the task modification is activating some effective strategy or process that neither group uses normally, or that, given the standard task, not all members of the proficient group use the process activated by the compensatory task. As Rohwer points out, the second interpretation is more plausible for outcomes where, although benefiting from the compensatory condition, the proficient group does no better than the improficient group on the modified task. When the two groups differ under both versions of the task, there remains both the possibility that the task modification may not be directly related to the process responsible for the group difference on the standard task and the possibility that equivalent treatment conditions have not been provided.

We can illustrate the interpretive dilemma posed by such less-than-ideal outcomes with some data obtained by Scribner and Cole (1972). Previous findings that older children recall more than younger children from categorized recall lists had left the source of that age difference unclear. The interpretation of such findings was clouded both by the possibility that results were confounded by the sorts of inequivalencies so frequent in comparative research and by the common problem in cognitive investigations that performance differences do not in themselves reveal the underlying process differences that are of real interest to the researcher. In discussing a number of free recall clustering studies in chapter 2, we emphasized that the task clearly involves a large number of different steps or processes and that there is no general agreement as to what these processes are, let alone which ones are responsible for developmental differences in performance. Scribner and Cole administered two versions of the recall task to second, fourth, and sixth graders in order to ascertain whether these age groups differ in their use of a specific recall process — a categorical retrieval plan. To test this hypothesis, the two tasks had to be designed in such a way that any developmental differences in the way lists are stored in memory during the study trial and in accessibility to the category structure (category names) at the time of test could be ruled out as bases for group performance differences. (If younger children do not group items in categories as they learn them or cannot remember what categories were represented on the recall list at the time of test, they will not be able to organize a retrieval strategy around those categories.)

Scribner and Cole used two very similar versions of the recall task to fulfill these requirements. Both included using the same word lists, with randomized ordering of category members, and informing subjects before each study trial of the four categories of words that would appear on the list. The tasks differed only in the test procedure. In one version, the experimenter gave the child the category names again before the recall test and then instructed the child to recall as many words as she could ("Tell me all the things you can remember"). In the other version, the category names were again provided at test, but in this case the recall was constrained. The experimenter asked for recall category by category ("Tell me all the food you can remember"). If different age groups were to show equivalent recall levels on this constrained recall task, it would be hard to attribute differences in the first task to developmental differences in familiarity with the items, organization of the list during the study trial, or accessibility of list cues. However, the results Scribner and Cole actually obtained did not conform to a clearly interpretable developmental pattern. Age groups differed on both tasks. Moreover, constraining subjects' recall in the second task led to better performance than in the first task for sixth graders as well as for younger children. Hence, requiring subjects to use a categorical retrieval plan appeared facilitative for all ages tested, but age differences in propensity to use such a plan when not constrained to employ it (that is, in the first task) were not established as the source of developmental differences in cued recall. The study's design would have allowed such an inference if the ideal outcome had been attained, but the actual results left the locus of developmental differences in cued recall open. They could stem from differences in organization of the items into categories during the study trial, in rehearsal processes, in attention, in familiarity with the items or categories, or from a combination of these factors.

The important point is that in the frequent cases where a less-than-ideal outcome is obtained in a Group × Task study, we are left not with a single, convincing account for group differences but with the need to conduct more studies to try to locate the bases for group differences. A major difficulty in using a Group × Task design to study group processing differences is that such less-than-ideal outcomes are more common than the idealized result required for an unambiguous interpretation. After all, one would expect that given a cognitive task, younger and older children or normal and retarded individuals would differ in not just one way but in several (see Chi, 1978). The problem is that when a task modification designed to compensate for a particular difference improves performance in the less proficient subjects but falls short of bringing them up to the level of the more proficient, we do not know if we have some additional processing differences to account for, or a problem of treatment inequivalence, or a combination of the two. We can keep modifying our compensatory task to try to compensate for additional processing differences (as Scribner and Cole did), but unless we can get equivalent performances from the two groups on some version of the task, we will be unable to draw any clear inference.

Rohwer points out that even when a perfectly hypothesis-consistent outcome is attained, several steps remain to be carried out.

To begin with, the finding should be replicated, making sure that the failure of the task modification to improve performance for those learners who are proficient on the standard task is not due to the fact that they are already performing at the top of the response scale and hence have no room to show improvement; or, if the task modification is a change in instructions, that they simply have not complied with the modified instructions. In addition, if the task modification involves a strong form of compensation, actually giving the subject whatever it is that is presumed to result from activating the process of interest (for example, *giving* the subjects elaborative sentences for each pair), the experimenter should investigate whether some weaker intervention that merely induces subjects to employ the process within the task (for instance, instructing them to make up sentences linking nouns) will suffice. Rohwer refers to these two sorts of compensation as *prosthetic* and *catalytic*; the first is relevant to assumptions about lack of ability, the second to hypotheses about lack of propensity to employ available strategies, processes, or structures.

Another step commonly used to strengthen the case for a specific hypothesis about group differences is to modify the standard task in some other way in order to make the performance of the proficient group resemble that of the improficient. The rationale for this is that if the advantage of the proficient group on the standard task stems from the use of some specific process or strategy, and if the task is modified to prevent the members of the group from using that strategy, their performance should resemble that of the improficient group. Since the improficient presumably do not employ the process anyway, preventing its use in the modified task should not affect their performance.

Training Studies

Training studies designed to raise the level of an improficient group of learners to that of a standard proficient group constitute the third approach to comparative research. Like the Group × Task approach, this one is based on an analysis of the components of the task under study and upon hypotheses about group differences in propensity or ability to carry out one or more of those component processes. If young children do more poorly on serial recall tasks than older children, for example, and we hypothesize that their relative deficit originates from a failure to cumulatively rehearse the study items as they are presented, we might seek to corroborate this hypothesis by training young children to rehearse and then looking for improvement in their serial recall.[5]

The training study approach is actually quite closely related to the more general Group × Task approach, and often the two strategies will both be employed within a given research program. A protracted effort at training improficient subjects is generally reasonable only after the deficit of that group (or at least *a* deficit) has been located, and one prominent means for pinpointing the locus of a deficit is through a Group × Task type of analysis. There are several differences between the two approaches, however. While any theoretically relevant task modification may be used in the Group × Task strategy for uncovering some process on which the groups differ, the sorts of task modifications employed in a training study are by definition limited to those involving direct instruction on how to perform some component of the task. Modifications of task materials or changes in instructions that serve merely to clarify the nature of the task would not qualify as training (Belmont and Butterfield, 1977) although such modifications are frequently used within a Group × Task strategy. Training studies are also characterized by the use of longer, more elaborate instructional procedures since they are conceptualized as *teaching* subjects to perform some process or strategy, rather than simply stimulating them to employ a strategy they are already capable of carrying out or providing a prosthesis for something they do not have. Another difference is that compensatory training is usually provided only for the improficient group. This procedure may seem reasonable from a strictly pragmatic standpoint since training may be costly and time-consuming and because the standard group is already performing at a level considered proficient. Thus, while the Group × Task approach requires a minimum of four groups (proficient group with standard task; proficient group with modified task; improficient group with standard task; improficient group with modified task), a training study by definition employs two groups — improficient group with training, and improficient group with no training. A third — proficient group with no training — is sometimes dispensed with when a difference between the two comparison groups has been established in previous research. Use of what would be the fourth group in a Group × Task design (proficient subjects given the training) is even less common. Failure to include this group in the research design means sacrificing an important source of corroboration for the assumption that what we are teaching is in fact the process that proficient learners typically employ on the task in question. It is quite possible, in fact, that we are teaching some procedure that would lead members of the standard group to perform at higher levels also.

Any training procedure will involve many factors, making it difficult to locate the source of an obtained improvement. When a group of proficient learners receiving training is not included in the design, the nature of the facilitation produced by training is even harder to pinpoint. The picture is complicated further by the fact that subjects using different strategies may attain equivalent levels of performance, and there may be differences both among the various individuals within a given group and within a single individual in regard to the strategies that are used in a particular task.

To combat these problems, researchers need some performance-independent measure of the process or strategy they are trying to teach. By measuring the cognitive activity that we believe is responsible for differences in group performance, we can ascertain the degree to which such activity is common in proficient learners and rare in improficient learners under standard task conditions. The experimenter also gains a means of indexing the degree to which the training procedure successfully instills this process or strategy in the improficient. And in addition, what may appear to be inconsistencies in the data, such as slow learners improving without training or members of the proficient group performing poorly, may be checked to see if these inconsistencies are explainable in terms of differences in the use of the relevant process or strategy (as when some members of the slow group generate the strategy without instruction, and some members of the generally proficient group do not employ it). In a training study that does not employ the full four-group factorial design, such a measure is a key factor in interpreting training effects in terms of processes of interest.

Though arguing for the promise of this research strategy, Belmont and Butterfield have been careful to point out the difficulties involved. As already noted, this approach is dependent upon an analysis of the task under study and on the experimenter's knowledge of the strategies and processes used by efficient learners. Motivational problems or failure on the part of some subjects to fully comply with instructions are factors that frequently impair the efficacy of training.

The researcher must be alert to *differential mortality* among groups, in which more subjects tend to drop out of some conditions than out of others for reasons related to the experimental treatment. For example, in a study of the effects of training retarded subjects on a cognitive process, the subjects having the most trouble mastering the task might drop out of the study, either by not attending sessions or by no longer making an effort to follow the directions. The subjects remaining in the training condition, then, would be those who were more motivated and possibly even somewhat more skilled to begin with. If no such differential dropping-out has happened in the control group, the results will make the effectiveness of the training look artificially high. Differential mortality is most likely to occur in training studies that cover a long time period, and it can be a serious threat to interpretability of results. It is always wise to examine and report mortality rates in ruling out alternative explanations of data.

Cognitive research with retardates provides some of the best illustrations of the training study approach. Research conducted by Ann Brown and her colleagues will be used as a case study. (For other good examples, see Butterfield, Wambold, and Belmont, 1973; or Butterfield and Belmont, 1977.) The research involved a "keeping track" task. During each one of a series of trials, the subject is shown sequentially a number of items that are members of different categories (for example, a food followed by an animal, an article of clothing, and a vehicle). The same set of categories is used on each trial, but the category order and the particular instances differ. Table 4.1 illustrates a series of eight consecutive trials from such a task. After viewing the set of items on a trial, the subject has to name the last item seen in a category selected by the experimenter ("What was the last food you saw?"). Previous research had shown that older children and adults performed well on this task regardless of the number of different instances of each category included on the task trials. Preschool children, however, did better on the task when there were fewer instances of each category (for example, when the last

Table 4.1. A "keeping track" task.

Trial	Presentation cycle				Category probe question
1	apple	dress	car	dog	What was the last *food?*
2	airplane	cake	mouse	pants	What was the last *animal?*
3	shoe	car	rabbit	bread	What was the last *food?*
4	cow	pants	airplane	cookie	What was the last *clothing?*
5	car	cat	apple	coat	What was the last *vehicle?*
6	shoe	bread	horse	airplane	What was the last *food?*
7	rabbit	car	dress	cake	What was the last *clothing?*
8	cookie	dog	airplane	coat	What was the last *animal?*

food might be "apple" or "cake" rather than when it could be "apple," "cake," "bread," or "cookie"). Brown (1972) found this same effect for retarded adolescents: retardates were better at keeping track of the last instance of a category seen when there were only two instances of the category than when there were four or six. Brown suggested that retardates perform as if they are searching through their memory for all the instances of a category that are being used in the task, looking for the one they saw most recently. The fewer the items from the category (and hence the fewer the "time tags" the subject has to confront), the easier such recency discriminations should be. Normal adolescents, on the other hand, appear to be just rehearsing the four items on each trial ("apple, dress, car, dog") and selecting the one that fits the category asked for by the experimenter. If a subject actively rehearses just the items included on the current trial, the number of different instances of a given category that appear throughout the task will not be important in determining performance. Accordingly, Brown, Campione, Bray, and Wilcox (1973) reasoned that it is the failure of retardates to rehearse the four items during each trial that accounts for their poor performance when more than two instances of a category are used in the keeping-track task. They hypothesized that training retardates to rehearse in that way should both improve their general accuracy in the task and wipe out the detrimental effect of using a larger number of instances of a category.

To fit this experiment within the context described above, two groups (improficient learners with no training; improficient learners with training) were tested. The qualitative and quantitative character of the performance of the standard group (proficient learners with no training) had been established in previous research. The effect of the number of category instances on performance was taken as a measure of the process or strategy being used: subjects whose performance suffered when more instances were used in the task were presumed to be searching through all the presented members of a category for the most recently seen instance, and subjects who showed no such effect were presumed to be cumulatively rehearsing just the instances seen on the latest trial. Adolescent retardates were given fifteen days of testing on the keeping-track task. Sixteen pictures from the categories of food, clothing, animals, and vehicles were used, with each set of materials containing two instances for one category, four instances for two, and six instances for one, as in table 4.1. After a day of becoming familiar with the materials and the task, the experimental subjects were given four days of training in cumulatively rehearsing the items on each trial of the keeping-track task. Control subjects were given the task with no special instructions. During the rest of the experiment, the subjects were given twenty-four trials each day, and those who had been trained in rehearsal were prompted to continue rehearsing. Performance on these final trials was in accord with predictions. The subjects trained to cumulatively rehearse performed more accurately than the control subjects and were not adversely affected by the number of instances in a category. The untrained subjects, on the other hand, performed more poorly on the one category with six instances than on the two categories with four, and their performance on these two categories was worse than on the single two-instance category. Brown et al. also gathered other types of rehearsal measures to bolster their conclusion that the training produced cumulative rehearsal. Their nonrehearsal subjects did better if the experimenter asked for a category instance that had been the last item seen during the trial (a recency effect), while the cumulative rehearsal-trained subjects did just as well on earlier items as on the final item within the trial. The time that nonrehearsal subjects took to respond to the category probe question varied with the number of category instances and with the position of the item in the series, but this was not so for subjects trained to rehearse.

The strategy of trying to make proficient learners perform like improficient ones was also employed within this series of studies. In a second experiment, Brown et al. administered the keeping-track task to ninth graders of normal IQ. For half of these subjects, the experimenters tried to block the cumulative rehearsal that was assumed to be the spontaneous strategy of ninth graders. The method for doing so was to train these subjects to overtly (audibly) repeat the name of the last-displayed item until the next item appeared. As expected, subjects in this repetition condition performed like untrained retardates in the previous experiment. Their performance was relatively poor, and it deteriorated as the number of category instances increased. Subjects who were free to perform the task in their own way, on the other hand, were unaffected by the number of instances, were more accurate, and responded faster than the repetition subjects.

In line with the argument made earlier, this research illustrates the importance of having some way to measure the strategy that subjects are using—in this case taking the effect of the number of category instances on performance as a measure of rehearsal. If such a measure had not been available, it would have been quite difficult to interpret the positive result of the training procedure. If only overall performance accuracy had been measured, one could argue that the trained retardates did better on the posttraining trials not because they were cumulatively rehearsing but because the training had increased their motivation, attention, or verbalization of items. One could also suggest that while cumulative rehearsal might be a useful strategy in the keeping-track task, it is not necessarily the strategy used by normal subjects. Requiring ninth graders to repeat aloud the last item presented would disrupt any number of strategies, not just cumulative rehearsal. Thus, the support for the process interpretation of these results would have been very weak if it had not been for the presence of a measure of the subjects' strategy. Because of the lack of a critical comparison group in such training studies (proficient learners that have been given the training), it is essential to obtain a measure of the process supposedly being trained.

Although we have stressed the importance of measures of component processes or task strategies in disambiguating the results of comparative studies, we're not under the illusion that we are offering a simple solution to basic design problems. Devising satisfactory measures of task processes or strategies is one of the most challenging problems in contemporary cognitive research. Many of the measures that have been used rest on unproved assumptions. As Belmont and Butterfield point out, what is wanted is as direct a measure as possible of the process under study, in terms both of the amount of logical inference involved and the point at which the measure is taken. In the comparative case studies we have discussed so far, both the effect of the number of categories in the keeping-track task and the difference between standard and elaboration conditions in the paired-associate task are relatively indirect measures of the processes of interest. More direct measures of various processes have been devised; for example, subjects are sometimes instructed to rehearse aloud. But such procedures force us to worry about the possibility that the conditions devised to make the cognitive activity accessible to measurement have some unintended effect on that activity. For instance, there is some evidence that requiring overt rehearsal affects the way subjects perform in a memory task (Kellas, McCauley, and McFarland, 1975). In like manner, asking a subject to describe aloud what he is doing in order to remember each pair of nouns of a paired-associate list may lead him to use elaboration to a greater extent than he normally would, or may influence the types of elaborations he generates — perhaps stimulating verbal rather than imaginal elaborations, or making him feel constrained to produce elaborations with a certain degree of elegance, rationality, or creativity. To avoid this kind of contamination of task performance, such measures are often taken after the task is completed (for example, by asking the subject to go back over a paired-associate list he has learned and indicate how he learned each pair). Although posttest probing of processes eliminates the danger of unintended influences on performance measures, it is open to challenges regarding its accuracy (see Nisbett and Wilson, 1977). When asked to report any elaborations after the fact, for example, subjects may have forgotten some they actually used, may generate elaborations for pairs they learned by rote in order to have something to say for every pair, or may again feel constrained to make their elaborations fit some perceived criterion of "goodness."

Thus, the degree to which a measure of a process or strategy is a *direct* measure is an important factor in evaluating cognitive research. Experimenters will not always agree about what constitutes a reasonably direct measure. For instance, serial position curves showing better memory for the first few items in a recall list than for middle-list items (primacy effect) are commonly used to index rehearsal since most theoretical explanations for this advantage for initial items attribute it to greater opportunities for rehearsing them. However, Belmont and Butterfield object to using the primacy effect as a measure of rehearsal since there are other possible explanations for it. They are willing, however, to accept the amount of time the subject spends on each item in a self-paced task as a direct measure of the amount of rehearsal he engages in. Yet clearly, this measure is based on inference also; we cannot be sure what the subject is doing with his study time. Moreover, a ten-second interval between list items may not mean the same thing for a first grader as for a sixth grader; it may take a first grader a longer time to generate the same number of rehearsals. The use of spontaneous overt verbalization as a measure of rehearsal (Keeney, Cannizzo, and Flavell, 1967) is fairly unambiguous as an indication that rehearsal has occurred, but we cannot assume that rehearsal *has not* occurred just because the subject does not say the list words out loud. Moreover, older subjects are more likely than younger ones to do their rehearsing covertly. The ambiguity of another measure, free recall clustering, which is often interpreted as a measure of process, was discussed earlier. In light of the imperfect quality of most such process measures, Brown and Campione (1977) recommend using more than one measure whenever possible. This strategy was illustrated in the Brown et al. study just described. In addition, continuing efforts to devise experimental means of measuring basic processes more directly should be encouraged because the payoffs for interpretability of cognitive research are great.

Cautionary Notes

The three strategies described in this chapter have been developed as a means of ameliorating the conceptual problems posed by comparative research. However, utilization of one of these strategies is not guaranteed to resolve the difficulties of comparative research. The strategies are all dependent on the quality of the researcher's task analysis and on obtaining a certain set of outcomes in order to yield clear inferences about group differences in cognitive functioning. When the within-group patterns of effects are different for two cultures, ages, or species, we can only conclude that the groups employ different processes under the specific — and not necessarily equivalent — conditions we have instituted in our experiment. When two groups do not perform equally well on the compensatory task in a Group × Task design, we cannot be sure whether the problem is that other processes are involved in the more proficient group's superiority or whether our treatment conditions are not really equivalent for the two groups. A training procedure must demonstrate its efficacy not only in raising the level of task performance but also in effecting the activation of the specific process hypothesized to produce group performance differences, if inferences about cognitive processing are to be made.

These efforts may be complicated by the fact that processes involved in performing a task are interdependent, in that they all draw upon a limited supply of mental resources. In order to execute a cognitive task successfully, an individual must be able not only to perform each component of the task, but also to perform all of them together. A number of psychologists have suggested that human performance is subject to a basic limit on mental resources or the number of mental operations that can be executed together (see, for example, Norman and Bobrow, 1975; Shatz, 1977). Thus in many cases, an individual may fail to carry out a component process not because he is incapable of performing it but because he lacks sufficient resources to do it *and* to do all the other components of the task as well.

A limitation on the resources available for allocation among various task components would have serious repercussions for the kinds of Group × Task and training designs discussed in this chapter. In these analyses, the various processes involved in the task are considered as independent components. If we have hypothesized that young children do not execute some process (for example, elaboration) and we provide training or a prosthetic device for it, we assume that any improvement in performance is a product of that process. Thus, our whole strategy for isolating the processes involved in group differences is predicated on the assumption that our intervention is affecting a single task component. If task components all draw upon a limited fund of resources, any factor that affects the amount of resources required to execute one will also have an impact on others.

Research described by Resnick and Glaser (1976) on teaching children the operation of "carrying" used in addition illustrates this situation. Wooden blocks, designed to represent numerical quantity, were used to teach the place-value system and the skills needed to carry. Blocks were displayed in three-column arrays with hundred-unit squares in the first column, ten-unit bars in the second column, and single-unit cubes in the third. Initially, for one group of children, each column contained from one to nine blocks and the children were taught to assign numerals representing the number of blocks in each column. Next they were taught how to exchange blocks of different sizes. For example, ten one-cubes could be exchanged for one ten-bar. After these two task components (notation of numerals and exchange of different-sized units) were learned, the researchers tested to see if the children could correctly coordinate the two operations. They were given arrays where some columns had more than nine blocks and exchanges had to be performed before assigning one-digit numerals. Interestingly, children who had executed the exchange routine quite well when that was the only thing they had to do started making exchange errors. For instance, when there were fourteen blocks in the ones column, they typically would remove ten of these and assign the digit four, but would fail to add a ten-bar to the next column in compensation. Their problem appeared not to be an inability to exchange, but an inability to perform the exchange within the context of a larger task that placed additional demands on their mental resources.

The interdependence of task components was illustrated in another way by the performance of a second group of children in this study. These children had the same instruction as those in the first group with one additional feature: during the notation training they sometimes had columns with more than nine blocks. They were told that since only a one-digit number could be assigned, they did not know how to solve these problems yet. These children, then, were trained to check a problem first to see if it was solvable. Following exchange training, they were given the same chance to coordinate notation and exchange as the other group. The outcome was that children trained to check a column before assigning a numeral did not make the same kind of exchange errors as children in the other group. If they had to remove ten blocks from the ones column, they added a ten-bar to the next column in compensation. Training on one component of the task (checking to see if a one-digit number could be assigned) apparently facilitated the execution of another (exchange) when the whole task of carrying was attempted. This result makes sense if it is assumed that as any one task component becomes more automatic and takes up less of the subject's mental resources, the performance of other components will improve. The resource-dependence of task components makes pinpointing the processes responsible for group differences much more difficult.

5.

Model-based Approaches

In model-based research, subjects' performance on a task of interest is compared to an explicit, detailed theoretical model of the various component processes involved in executing the task. In chapter 2, FRAN, the free recall model developed by Anderson and Bower, was used to illustrate the use of a simulation model in noncomparative research. In this chapter, various types of models that have been employed in comparative research will be described. The four model categories discussed—qualitative information processing models, computer simulation models, mathematical models, and functional measurement—differ in form and in the details of their application to comparative research. All, however, share the rationale that developing a system that can reproduce subjects' intellectual performance is a promising strategy for gaining a better understanding of the factors underlying their thinking.

The logic of model-based approaches when applied to comparative research is as follows. Using cognitive theory, empirical observation, or logical induction, the researcher sets up a model of the way proficient learners solve the task under study, as well as models for various types of alternative systems that might be applied by less sophisticated subjects. After these hypothetical performance models have been generated, the "output" of each model (whether derived through logical deduction, mathematics, or computer simulation) is compared with the actual task performance of each group of subjects. Then the researcher can assess the proportion of subjects in each group that appears to employ a given task performance model and can base inferences about group differences in cognitive processing on the differences between the models.

Model-based approaches have proved to be useful in comparative research not only because they have generated detailed analyses of the components of successful performance for such important cognitive tasks as conservation, counting, and causal reasoning but also because they have focused attention on the need to understand the reasoning of less proficient subjects and to model their performance as well. In the field of developmental psychology, Brown and DeLoache (1978) have contrasted the strength of model-based research in this regard with what they consider to be the weakness of the typical developmental investigation of memory strategy.

The typical experiment in this area consists of crude assessments of the presence or absence of strategic intervention. Children are then divided into those who produce and those who do not; those who produce outperform those who do not. We rarely have evidence of intermediate stages of production . . . Probably the most important deficiency . . . is that the tasks are set up in such a way that we cannot say anything about nonproducers. If children are not rehearsing on our task, we have no way of knowing what it is they are doing.

They perform poorly and therefore they highlight the improvement with age we wish to demonstrate. However, we know nothing about their state of understanding. They are characterized as *not* being at a certain level, as *not* having a certain attribute; they are nonproducers, nonmediators; they are not strategic or not planful. They are sometimes described as passive, even though the tasks are designed so that the only way to be characterized as active is to produce the desired strategy. All these descriptions are based on what young children do not do compared with older children, for we have no way of observing what they *can* do in the confines of these tasks.   (pp. 7-8)

By generating and testing a model of the younger child's task performance, the model-based approach can offer a picture of what this child *can* do.

Qualitative Information-processing Models

The first type of model-based strategy, what we are calling a qualitative information-processing model, consists of an explicit specification of the sequence of steps a person carries out as he performs some task of interest. Different models of performance for the same task can be devised to reflect individual and group differences in the way the task is accomplished.

One of the most elegant examples of the use of this kind of model in comparative psychology is the series of studies performed by Siegler (1976) on children's performance with balance-scale problems. Siegler chose to study the balance-scale problem for three reasons: it embodies the mathematically interesting concept of proportionality; it had been used by Piaget to test for the attainment of formal operations; and enough was known about it empirically to suggest that development of knowledge relevant to the problem occurs over a large age range. A balance scale was used that had four pegs arranged at equal intervals on each side of its fulcrum (see figure 5.1). Children were asked to predict which side of the scale would go down when varying numbers of metal weights (of equal weight) were placed on each side and the wooden blocks under the scale arms were removed.

Siegler developed a model for mature performance on this task through rational task analysis. He also developed three models of less mature responding based on the empirical findings of earlier research with children. These four models, which Siegler termed Rules I-IV, are shown in figure 5.2. A child using Rule I pays attention only to the number of weights on each side of the scale. The respective distances of the weights from the fulcrum are ignored. The child predicts that

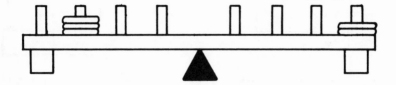

Model predictions and reasons

Rule I	Left side down (more weight)
Rule II	Left side down (more weight)
Rule III	Chance responding (conflict)
Rule IV	Left side down $(3 \times 3) > (4 \times 2)$

Figure 5.1. "Conflict" balance-scale problem. Based on Siegler, 1976.

the side with more weights will go down, or if both sides have the same number of weights, that the scale will balance. Rule II involves some consideration of distance, but only when the number of weights is the same on both sides. When the weights are equal, the user of Rule II shifts his attention to distance and predicts that the side with weights farther from the fulcrum will go down. The Rule III child, in contrast, always takes both weight and distance into account, but when one side has more weights and the other has its weights farther from the fulcrum, he has no rule for resolving the conflict. Rule IV, which represents the "mature" solution for the problem, differs from Rule III in its incorporation of a rule for resolving conflicts: the product of the distance and weight for each peg is calculated, and the sum for the right side is compared with

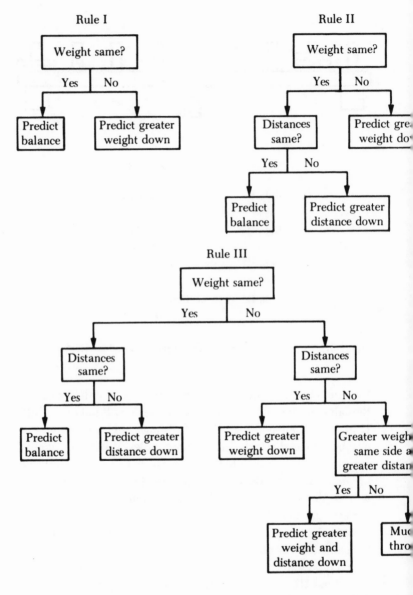

Figure 5.2. Siegler's rule models for the balance-scale task. From Siegler, 1976, pp. 484-485, figs. 2a-2d.

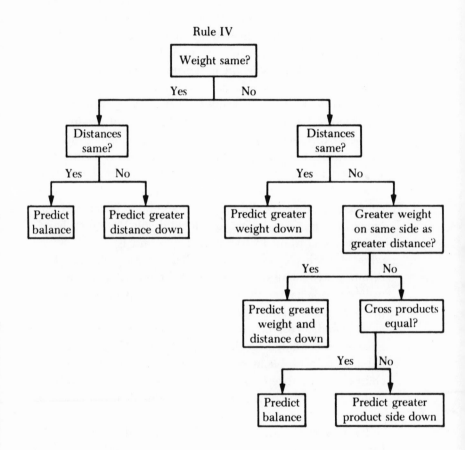

that for the left (for example, $(2 \times 3) + (3 \times 3) = 15$; $(3 \times 2) + (5 \times 1) = 11$; $15 > 11$). The Rule IV user predicts that the side with the larger sum of cross products will do down. Earlier research had indicated that many sixteen-year-olds are not aware of the formal rules contained in the Rule IV model.

After the task analysis, the next crucial step in this approach is setting up the task in such a way that one can determine which strategy each individual subject is using. Siegler did so by selecting balance-scale problems that would produce different performance patterns for children employing different rule systems. For example, one problem type was included for which young children using Rule I or II should do better than older children using Rule III. When weight and distance cues conflict, the Rule III child simply guesses and hence performs inconsistently. The Rule I or II child, on the other hand, responds according to the weight cue and ignores distance when given this type of problem. Therefore on problems where distance favors one side and weight the other, with the more weighted side having the larger sum of cross products as in the problem depicted in figure 5.1, the Rule I or II child will always predict correctly while the Rule III child will show only chance responding. Siegler selected six different types of balance-scale problems of such a nature that an individual child's performance over multiple trials on the various types would reveal which, if any, of the hypothetical rules she was using.

The series of balance-scale problems was administratered to five-, nine-, thirteen-, and seventeen-year-old girls. The psychological plausibility of the rule models was demonstrated by the fact that of the 120 girls tested, 107 could be classified according to the rule system they were using (on the criterion that 20 out of 24 responses were predicted by the relevant model). There were large developmental differences in the particular rules used: Rule I was followed by the large majority of five-years-olds, Rules II and III were used more by seventeen-year-olds than by younger subjects, and only eight subjects used Rule IV. After predictions had been made on the entire series of problems, the girls were asked to explain verbally the way in which they had solved the problems. When these explanations were classified, they matched the rules inferred from the performance measures for over 90 percent of the subjects.

The second experiment in this series involved training children to use a more advanced rule. Groups of five- and eight-year-olds, all of whom employed Rule I during pretesting, were given training designed to foster development of either Rule II or Rule III. The training consisted of problems for most of which Rule I was inadequate while the rule being trained (either Rule II or Rule III) was sufficient, along with feedback after each prediction — the wooden blocks beneath the scale arms were removed so that the child could see which arm actually did go down. A posttest without feedback showed that girls of both ages benefited from training that aimed at one step above their current knowledge level (Rule II, which requires that distance be considered only when there are equal numbers of weights on the two sides), but that only eight-year-olds were able to benefit from training geared to a higher level (Rule III, which requires considering distance for every problem). Although children at both ages apparently started with the same kind of knowledge about the problem, the older ones gained more from the training experience. The question that Siegler attacked next was what it was about the eight-year-olds that made them better able to profit from the Rule III training than the five-year-olds.

Observations of the younger children's behavior during training and testing suggested the hypothesis that they were less likely to adequately encode the distance dimension on balance-scale problems. A means for testing this notion was used in a third experiment. Children were shown various balance-scale problems and asked not to make predictions but to study the arrangement of weights so that they could produce it on a second scale after the model was hidden from sight. In line with the hypothesis, eight-year-olds were adept at making reproductions of the presented scale configurations that were equally accurate in terms of number of weights used and distance of the weights from the fulcrum. The performance of five-year-olds, on the other hand, was relatively accurate on the weight dimension but much poorer on distance. Subsequent experiments indicated that the five-year-olds' failure to encode the distance variable was not an artifact of time pressures or of misunderstanding the instructions.

Next, children were given explicit training on how to encode both the weight and the distance dimensions. They were taught to count both the weights and the pegs and then to include both pieces of information in a verbal description ("four weights on the third peg and five weights on the second peg"). After training, the five-year-olds' reproductions were as accurate on the weight as on the distance dimension. At the completion of encoding training, these subjects still were at the Rule I level when asked to predict which side of the scale would go down. Siegler next gave the children who had had encoding training the same Rule III prediction training used in the earlier experiment. This time, five-year-olds benefited from the training as much as eight-year-olds. Thus Siegler was able to demonstrate that group differences in reaction to training could be explained in terms of differences on an important component process (encoding).

The latter portion of this experimental series can be considered a variant of two approaches described in chapter 4 — Group × Task interaction and training. When a group difference phenomenon was obtained (differential effectiveness of Rule III training for the two ages), an attempt was made to relate that difference to group differences on some explanatory process (encoding). Training on the process of interest was given to both age groups in order to try to decrease the five-year-olds' failures to encode the distance dimension. It was then shown that encoding training was sufficient to overcome the overall age differences in responsiveness to Rule III training.

This portion of Siegler's research is impressive. Nevertheless, the approach illustrated by the first part of these studies is more relevant to our description of model-based research. The use of a detailed task analysis with explicit descriptions of rule systems at various stages of development was a crucial feature. This analysis was coupled with a structuring of the task in such a way that the strategy used by individual subjects could be uncovered. With this approach, we are not confined to analyses of differences between groups defined on the basis of a demographic index but can explore simultaneously the differences between users of different types of rule systems and any interactions that may exist between age and the way a particular rule system is employed. Moreover, this approach allows us to say not just that older subjects do better on balance-scale problems than younger subjects, but to describe the ways in which various subjects perform differently. The same rules assessment approach has been applied by Siegler to analyses of children's causal reasoning (Siegler, 1975), judgments of relative fullness (Siegler and Vago, 1978), Piaget's projection-of-shadows task, and a probability reasoning task (Siegler, 1978).

Computer Simulation Models

Computer simulation, like Siegler's qualitative task analysis, is an information-processing approach aimed at modeling the subject's performance as a temporally ordered sequence of steps. The difference between the two types of models lies in the simulation model's greater degree of detail, which is required because it has to be stated precisely enough to run on a digital computer. This stipulation not only encourages the researcher to model task performance at a very fine-grained level but also provides a means for objectively generating the output of the model system. As Klahr (1976) has put it, "In this way the implications of the total rule set can be unambiguously derived and compared to the child's actual behavior" (p. 100). It is the prevailing assumption of researchers employing this strategy that such highly detailed models of task performance are required in order to understand human behavior in a particular cognitive domain and eventually to understand how task performance changes over time as a function of practice, learning, or maturation.

Most of the comparative work with simulation models carried out thus far has aimed at providing models of performance for various Piagetian tasks by subjects at different stages of development and has been based on the general Newell and Simon (1972) information-processing approach developed in the study of complex problem solving by adults.

We will illustrate the computer simulation approach with an abbreviated description of a portion of the work performed by Baylor and Gascon (1974) on children's seriation of weight. Other examples of this type of research are described in Klahr (1976) and Klahr and Wallace (1970, 1976).

Weight seriation is one of a group of seriation tasks used by Piaget. In a seriation task the child is given an unordered array of objects that differ in terms of some physical dimension (say, sticks of varying lengths) and asked to order the items according to that dimension (put the sticks in a series proceeding from shortest to longest). To order the series correctly, the child must understand the transitivity of asymmetric relations (that is, that if stick A is longer than stick B, and stick B is longer than stick C, then stick A is longer than C), a logical understanding that younger children lack, according to Piaget.

The weight seriation task is analogous to the length task. Baylor and Gascon gave children ranging in age from six to twelve years seven cubes varying in weight but identical in appearance except for an arbitrary letter painted on each as an identifying mark. The children were also given a two-pan balance scale with which to weigh the blocks. They were instructed to order the blocks from heaviest to lightest, and their performance was videotaped. For each child, Baylor and Gascon then coded each move made in terms of which blocks were still in the original (unordered) problem set, which were on the scale, which of the two blocks being weighed was heavier, and which blocks were in the child's (supposedly ordered) answer set. From these protocols, simulation programs for different types of performance strategies characteristic of various stages of cognitive development were empirically derived.

The general characteristics of the performance of children at three different stages can be verbally described as follows.

The Stage 1 child weighs the blocks two at a time and, for each pair, puts the heavier block to the left of the lighter one and transfers the pair to the right end of the row constituting his answer set. The result is a juxtaposed set of pairs, with each odd-numbered item in the row being heavier than the even-numbered block to the right of it but with no coordination between the pairs. Using numbers to represent weight, a typical Stage 1 answer set might be 6, 3, 4, 1, 7, 2, 5.

The Stage 2 child is able to consistently order items within a subseries of three (or sometimes four) blocks, but does not order the various subseries. Her answer set is typically something of this sort: 7, 5, 2, 1, 6, 4, 3.

A child in the third stage performs at what Piaget terms the operational level and may use one of several strategies to solve the problem. One of these involves weighing all the blocks to find the heaviest and moving it into the first position in the answer set. Then each of the remaining blocks is weighed to find the heaviest among them, and that block is moved into the second position in the answer set, and so on. Each time the heaviest remaining block is located, all the lighter blocks are discarded into an unordered pool. Thus, although the strategy works, it is wasteful in that it requires much duplication of effort. A more elegant alternative is the "insertion strategy" in which the child systematically compares a block to be inserted into the answer set with those already in the series until he finds its proper position.

The computer simulation models for these stages are, of course, much more detailed and precise than these verbal descriptions. First, the child is characterized as having something called a knowledge system. A knowledge system includes a basic task strategy consisting of a hierarchically arranged set of goals. The ultimate objective of the system is to fulfill the highest goal in the hierarchy, which for this task is to put the weights in a series from heaviest to lightest (SERIATE). When such a higher-order goal is activated, the goal at the next level down in the hierarchy may be activated as a means for achieving the higher-order goal. Conversely, when a subgoal is satisfied, the system reactivates the goal at the higher level. Although the highest goal in the basic strategy for children at any of the stages described by Baylor and Gascon is to SERIATE the weights, children differ in terms of the lower-level or instrumental goals that serve to satisfy this objective. For example, the second-level goal for Stage 1 children is to find the heavy and light blocks in a pair, while for Stage 2 it is to find the heaviest in a subseries of three or four. Second-level goals at Stage 3 may be to find the heaviest block left in the problem set or to ascertain where to insert a block in the answer set.

The full goal hierarchy and the steps through which it is implemented will be described only for the simplest case of the

Stage 1 child. A full description of the simulation program for each stage may be found in Baylor and Gascon (1974).

As stated above, the Stage 1 child's goal hierarchy (or base strategy, as Baylor and Gascon call it) consists of the top-level goal of SERIATE capping a substructure designed to find the heavy and light members in a pair of blocks (FIND HEAVY AND LIGHT). This latter goal is in turn achieved by means of the lower-order goal WEIGH. When blocks have been put on the scale and the balance tips, the WEIGH goal is satisfied and the child moves the blocks off the scale into the answer set, satisfying the FIND HEAVY AND LIGHT goal. After this cycle of subgoals has been repeated for all the blocks in the problem set, the SERIATE goal itself is satisfied. This Stage 1 goal structure is diagramed in figure 5.3.

In order to translate this general goal structure into actual behavior (computer output), rules must be devised to relate the goals in the hierarchy to appropriate actions. The simulation program of Baylor and Gascon uses rules called *production systems* to meet this requirement (following Newell and Simon, 1972). A production system is a formal rule consisting of a specification of the combination of goal state and condi-

SERIATE

    FIND HEAVY AND LIGHT

      WEIGH

      Satisfy WEIGH

    Satisfy FIND HEAVY AND LIGHT

  Satisfy SERIATE

Figure 5.3. Goal hierarchy for Stage 1 model of weight seriation. The SERIATE cycle is repeated as many times as necessary until all items are out of the original problem set. Adapted from Baylor and Gascon, 1974, p. 8, fig. 2.

tions in the outside world (for example, the number of blocks in the scale pan) that will evoke the production system and the set of actions that the system performs. A production system's actions in turn modify conditions in the external world (for example, by moving blocks) and alter the system's goal state (by satisfying or activating goals), thus producing a new set of conditions that evokes a different production system.

Baylor and Gascon modeled the Stage 1 child's behavior in the weight seriation task as a set of seven production systems. Figure 5.4 shows these systems: the conditions necessary for evoking each one are listed in the left column and the associated actions in the right column.

At the beginning of the task, after instructions have been given and understood, the goal is to SERIATE the blocks, which are all still in their original unordered positions in the problem set. The conditions for P1 are thus satisfied and this production system is evoked, with the result that the goal is now set to FIND HEAVY AND LIGHT. Production systems P3-P5 all operate under the FIND HEAVY AND LIGHT goal, and the current external conditions are therefore critical in determining which of these production systems is evoked. When the child begins this task, no blocks are on the balance scale; so the conditions for P3 are satisfied, P3 is evoked, and the goal is set to WEIGH. When the goal is WEIGH, either P6 or P7 may be evoked depending on the number of blocks left to be seriated. At this point in the task solution, there are more than two blocks still in the problem set (all seven, in fact); so the activating conditions for P6 are satisfied. Two blocks are then taken from the right end of the problem set, one is placed in each scale pan, the scale tips toward the heavy member of the pair, and WEIGH is satisfied. As stated above, a basic feature of this type of system is that when the current goal is satisfied the next-higher goal in the hierarchy becomes active, which in this case is FIND HEAVY AND LIGHT. Since there are two blocks on the scale pans, P5 is

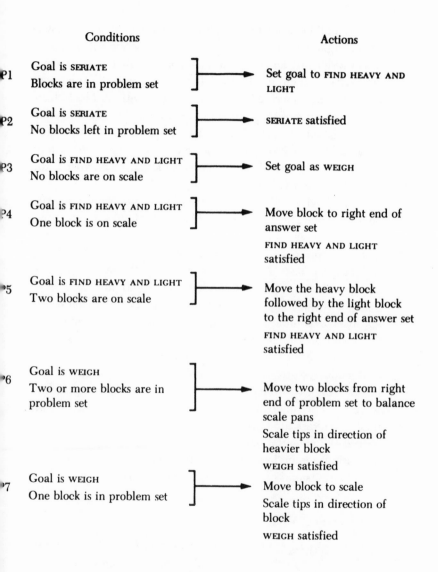

Figure 5.4. Production system model of Stage 1 weight seriation. Adapted from Baylor and Gascon, 1974, p. 14, fig. 3.

evoked and the heavy block, followed by the light one, is moved to the right end of the answer set. This action satisfies FIND HEAVY AND LIGHT and so the SERIATE goal automatically becomes active. Since there are blocks left to be seriated, P1 is evoked, and the cycle described above is repeated until all blocks have been moved out of the problem set, with the single modification that on the fourth cycle P7 and P4 are evoked rather than P6 and P5 because there is only one block left to be seriated. After four cycles, there are no blocks left to be seriated, P2 is evoked, the SERIATE goal is satisfied, and the system stops.

When Baylor and Gascon's various stage programs were run on a computer, the sequences of block moves given in their outputs were closely matched (and often identical) to those in the children's protocols from which they were derived. Future research that tests the programs' match to the performance of new samples of children of varying ages should provide an even more impressive test of the models. Further application of the approach to comparative research could also include comparing the proportion of children at different ages whose performance closely matches each of the stage models, singling out critical component processes as explanations for age differences, and training the less proficient learners in the use of these processes in a manner analogous to that employed by Siegler in his qualitative task analysis. Thus the simulation approach carries with it the potential benefits cited by Brown and DeLoache— increasing our understanding of the functioning of less proficient learners and providing guidelines for instruction.

Mathematical Models

A mathematical model of task performance represents component processes in the task as mathematical variables. The way in which processes are integrated is represented by a mathematical function combining those variables. The data generated by subjects actually performing the task are used to provide estimates for the parameters in the mathematical function. Some parameters may be directly measurable while others may be estimated by using a computer to generate the values of individual parameters that yield the "best fit" to the data. The differences between groups of subjects are represented as differences in parameter values. (This may, in effect, include "dropping out" some component process from the task model when the parameter representing it approaches the value of 0 or 1.)

A study of concept learning by Richard, Cauzinelle, and Mathieu (1973) illustrates the application of a mathematical model to comparative research. In this type of task the subject is given a series of trials in which he sees two stimuli varying from trial to trial along a number of different dimensions (for example, shape, color, position, and size). The subject indicates which stimulus he thinks is the right one on each trial before being told which one is correct. On the next trial he has two different stimuli differing along the same four dimensions and must again try to pick the right one. The subject's goal is to be able to make consistently right choices. As mentioned earlier, this task has been used in many studies concerned with intellectual development. Children, who typically perform less proficiently than adults, have been characterized as learning to solve the task through associations between individual stimuli and reward (for example, "the large red triangle is correct," and "the small red square is correct") rather than through concepts ("all red things are correct").

In their study of developmental differences in concept learning, Richard, Cauzinelle, and Mathieu made use of a technique developed by Levine (1966) for figuring out whether a subject is using a concept hypothesis to determine his choices, and if so, which of the possible hypotheses it is. The technique's logic is similar to that of Siegler's rule assessment.

For a particular set of concept learning items, we can identify in advance each of the values the subject might logically hypothesize is correct (for example, yellow, blue, small, large, triangle, circle, left, right). When two values of each dimension are used, a subject's choice on any one trial will be consistent with half of these hypotheses. If we give him a specially arranged set of trials without telling him whether he is right or wrong on these trials, we can determine from the pattern of responses over several trials which hypothesis he is using (assuming that he does not switch hypotheses under conditions of no feedback). Figure 5.5 contains an illustrative sequence of trials and shows the hypotheses that would be inferred from eight different patterns of subject responses. If, for example, the subject selected the large yellow circle on the first trial, the large yellow triangle on the second, the small yellow circle on the third, and the small yellow triangle on the fourth, the experimenters would conclude that the subject's hypothesis is that all yellow things are correct. When Richard and his colleagues used this technique, they found that performance appeared to be rule-governed in children just as in adults. Adults made responses indicating that they were using one of the hypotheses 90 percent of the time while children did so 88 percent of the time. The experimenters then applied a mathematical model of concept learning performance to the data from the subjects who performed as if they were using a concept hypothesis.

This model assumes that the subject has some hypothesis in mind (for example, "circle is correct") at the start of each trial and always selects the item in the pair of stimuli embodying this concept. The model then describes the way in which the subject changes his hypothesis over trials to arrive at the solution to the problem. One parameter of the model represents the probability that a subject beginning a trial with a particular hypothesis will not change his hypothesis if it is rein-

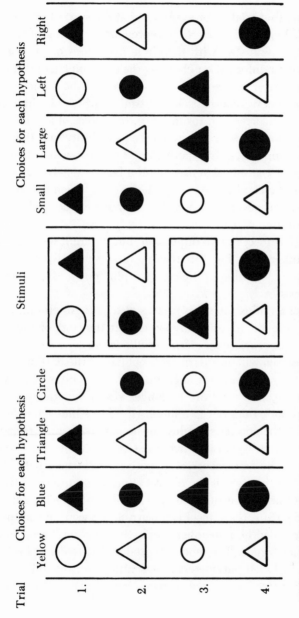

Figure 5.5. Response patterns consistent with each possible hypothesis in a concept learning task. Adapted from Richard, Cauzinille, and Mathieu, 1973, p. 318, table 3.

forced on that trial. (For example, if at the start of trial n the subject's hypothesis is *circle*, g represents the probability that the subject will stay with the circle hypothesis on trial $n+1$ after being reinforced for choosing the circle on trial n.) A second parameter is the probability, q, that the subject will switch to a new hypothesis after a trial on which his old hypothesis was incorrect. If, for instance, the choice of a circle was incorrect on trial n, q represents the probability that the subject will drop the circle hypothesis and pick a new one. The remainder of the model represents the factors determining the subset of the eight possible hypotheses from which the subject will select his new hypothesis. The stimuli were devised so that each item in a pair was similar to every other item in another pair with respect to two dimensions but different with respect to the other two. For this reason, three successive feedback trials are logically sufficient to pin down the correct hypothesis.

Figure 5.6 illustrates this process of hypothesis elimination. There are eight plausible hypotheses at the start of the task (*yellow, blue, triangle, circle, small, large, left, right*). One feedback trial will necessarily rule out half of these. (For example, if the small yellow triangle on the left is reinforced, *large, blue, circle,* and *right* are no longer viable hypotheses.) The next feedback rules out two more. (If a large blue triangle on the left is the correct stimulus on the next trial, only *triangle* and *left* are still plausible hypotheses.) A third feedback trial rules out the last incorrect hypothesis. (If the small blue triangle on the right is the correct stimulus on the third trial, the hypothesis *left* is ruled out and *triangle* must be the correct concept.) Thus, the subject can learn the concept in just three trials provided he remembers perfectly the stimuli reinforced on previous trials. The model devised by Richard and his colleagues included parameters representing the probability that the subject remembers the correct stimulus (1) from the most

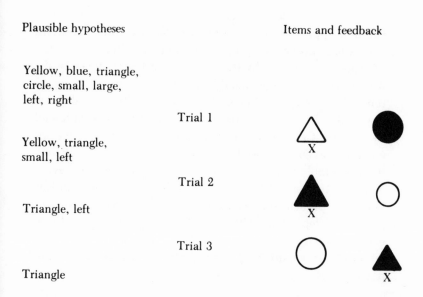

Plausible hypotheses   Items and feedback

Yellow, blue, triangle,
circle, small, large,
left, right

                              Trial 1

Yellow, triangle,
small, left

                              Trial 2

Triangle, left

                              Trial 3

Triangle

Figure 5.6. Hypothesis elimination after feedback trials in a concept learning task. An X indicates the correct stimulus.

recent feedback trial, (2) from the feedback trial before that, and (3) from the feedback trial twice removed. These researchers examined their subjects' performance to see if it was consistent with the reinforcement on the previous trial, with that on the previous two trials, and with that on the previous three trials after various patterns of positive and negative feedback. A computer was used to obtain the estimates for each probability in the model that would generate values most closely matching those obtained from the actual performance of children and adults. The obtained estimates suggested that both children and adults come close to the optimal strategy of always choosing a new hypothesis after negative feedback and never switching after positive feedback. Age differences on the memory parameters appeared to be larger, however. Although children appeared to remember the last reinforced stimulus with a high probability, they were much less likely to use the information provided by the results of earlier feedback trials. Adults, on the other hand, appeared to be as likely to remember (and use) the results from a feedback trial twice removed as from the most recent one. Thus the results obtained by Richard, Cauzinelle, and Mathieu suggest that the developmental difference in speed of solution for this type of task may be attributable to age differences in the component process of memory. It should be kept in mind, however, that with this kind of approach to comparative cognition, such conclusions are model-dependent. Other mathematical models could be generated to fit the same data, and with them the developmental difference would not necessarily be attributed to the same process.

Functional Measurement

Much of our discussion has emphasized the problems created for cognitive research by the fact that intellectual tasks almost always involve a number of different cognitive processes or activities, complicating the investigator's efforts to assess the role of any one process. An interesting approach to this dilemma is that of functional measurement, a research technique developed by Norman Anderson and his associates to cope with the problem of studying a subject's integration of different pieces of information to form an overall judgment. Anderson (1980) describes the need for such an approach:

Virtually all thought and behavior is multiply caused. Seldom does an external stimulus or internal force act alone, without being conditioned by the simultaneous operation of other forces. This basic fact of multiple causation is well known in every area of psychology, from perceptual judgments of size and distance, to social judgments of attractiveness or fairness.

But multiple causation is hard to study. Although innumerable investigators have been concerned with specific problems of stimulus integration and interaction, attempts at general theory have been rare. The reason is simple. When diverse causal forces are at work, each pushing in its own direction, the net resultant is difficult to predict and difficult to analyze. To pursue the analysis very far requires a quantitative theory of stimulus integration. That in turn requires a capability for measuring the subjective, psychological values of the stimuli. Lack of such a measurement capability has held back the study of stimulus integration. (p. 1)

The basic assumption underlying the functional measurement approach is that most human judgments will conform to some sort of simple algebraic model; the method involves testing for the psychological validity of various models while at the same time providing a means for measuring subjective values.

This method is applied to the modeling of human judgments that involve (at least potentially) the integration of two or more pieces of information. For example, subjects may be given a hypothetical scenario describing a person's intent and the severity of the consequences attending his actions and then be asked to judge how responsible that person was for the results described. The scenario might involve a married couple having a heated argument at the top of a flight of stairs, with one person (say, the husband) eventually tumbling down the stairs. Given information about the wife's intent and about the severity of the injuries suffered by the husband, subjects are asked to judge (and provide a numerical estimate for) the wife's responsibility for those injuries.

In attempting to integrate the two pieces of information (intent and consequences), subjects may either add them or multiply them. In the first case the algebraic function may be expressed as:

$$R = K + W_1 I + W_2 C$$

where R stands for judged responsibility, K is a constant, I is degree of harmful intent, C is severity of consequences, and W_1 and W_2 are subjects' weightings for these two factors. (Both factors need not be considered equally important; subjects may vary in the relative importance they assign to them in making responsibility judgments.) In the second case, when subjects see responsibility as a multiplicative function of intent and consequences, the algebraic function may be expressed as:

$$R = K + W_1 I \times W_2 C.$$

Hypothetical data conforming to these two models are depicted in figure 5.7. Many human judgments and perceptions seem to fit one of these models. In the present example, intent is factor 1 and three levels of severity of consequence compose factor 2. As the figure indicates, under the additive model the difference in judged responsibility between a wife having a high intent to harm her spouse and one having a medium intent to do so would be unaffected by the severity of consequence (by whether the husband suffered a sprained ankle or a broken neck). In the multiplicative model, however, the difference between the same two cases in judged responsibility is clearly dependent on the severity of consequences.[1]

As the idealized curves in figure 5.7 show, an additive model is associated with a set of parallel straight lines while the multiplicative model is associated with a set of diverging straight lines, which Anderson calls a "linear fan." The two models can be tested in an analysis of variance. Both additive and multiplicative models of information integration predict the main effects of consequences and intent. Under the multiplicative model, but not the additive model, a significant interaction between consequences and intent is expected.

A major advantage of the functional measurement technique is that it makes possible the derivation of a validated scale of subjective values of the perception or judgment under study. Anderson argues that the response data would not come

Additive Model

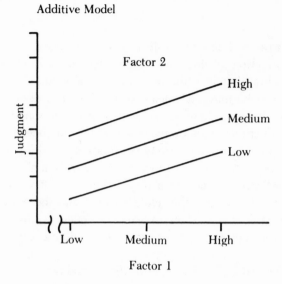

Multiplicative Model

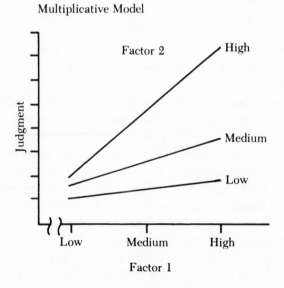

Figure 5.7. Factorial plots of hypothetical data conforming to additive and multiplicative models.

out as straight lines if a subject's overt responses were not a linear function of his underlying psychological responses. Hence, obtaining data that plot out as parallel lines or a linear fan allows the marginal means in the factorial design to be used as a linear scale of subjective values (Anderson, 1976).

The functional measurement technique has been successfully applied to a wide variety of situations, such as: predictions of performance as a function of motivation and ability; perceived attractiveness of a play group as a function of the characteristics of the other children in it and the number of toys available to it; evaluation of deservingness as a function of need and achievement; rated social desirability as a weighting of two adjectives describing a hypothetical person; and attitude toward a past president of the United States as a function of several provided pieces of information about him.

The method can be used within a comparative context to ascertain whether the way two pieces of information are integrated to reach a particular type of judgment differs for members of different groups. A developmental study of area and volume judgments by Anderson and Cuneo (1978) illustrates the use of the method within a comparative framework.

How children of varying ages integrate cues to judge the size of physical quantities is an interesting question both in its own right and in relation to Piagetian theory. Piaget developed the standard task for assessing conservation, the understanding that perceptual changes in a substance brought about by changing its shape or configuration do not alter its quantity. In the classic conservation-of-liquid task, the child is shown two identical beakers containing equal quantities of water. After confirming the fact that the two beakers contain the same amount of water, the child watches as the experimenter pours the water from one beaker into another beaker with a different shape, perhaps taller but with a smaller diameter. When asked to judge whether the two amounts are identical after this transformation, the child under seven typically responds negatively. He asserts that the amounts are no longer equal and judges that one beaker (usually the one with the higher water level) has more water. Until the age of seven or so, the child given this task does not appear to understand that such a perceptual transformation does not have an effect on liquid quantity. Typically, the young child performs analogously in logically identical experiments on other types of quantity, such as two balls of clay, one of which is flattened. According to Piaget the young child is unable to coordinate two dimensions at the same time to realize that the increase in height is compensated for by a decrease in width. The child is described as "centrating" on just one dimension and basing his quantity judgment on it.

Anderson and Cuneo's approach to the study of conservation was to treat it as an assessment of the young child's method for forming volume estimates. They pointed out an important limitation in the standard Piagetian task with regard to its ability to elucidate the child's strategy for judging volume. Asking the child to indicate which beaker contains "more" may reveal whether the nonconserving child regards height or width as a more important determinant of quantity, but it will not reveal whether the other dimension is completely ignored in the judgment process (as Piaget assumes) or simply plays a lesser role. It is possible that the young child realizes the column of liquid in the second beaker is narrower as well as taller but thinks that the increase in height more than makes up for the decrease in width.

Anderson and Cuneo's method for investigating quantity judgments involved having children of varying ages judge a whole series of liquid and solid quantities, rating each on a nineteen-point scale as to how happy that much "Kool-Aid" (or that big a cookie, or whatever) would make a thirsty (or hungry) child. The height and width dimensions were varied systematically, with each child judging the stimulus embodying each combination of the dimensions used in the experiments at least once, and in some studies twice. In this manner, it was possible to generate integration models fitting data at the level of the individual child as well as the level of the age group.

Thus far the logic may sound very similar to that underlying Siegler's research. However, instead of focusing on the qualitative pattern of judgments across different problem types as Siegler did, Anderson and Cuneo assessed their quantitative features by plotting ratings for each stimulus and testing the unidimensional, additive, and multiplicative models through analyses of variance. While the eleven-year-olds appeared to make volume judgments about liquids in a logically correct multiplicative fashion, five-year-olds' judgments were apparently based on height alone. Hence their responses were consistent with the Piagetian notion of centration.

Anderson and Cuneo wanted to test whether this unidimensional model was a characteristic general to all quantity judgments at that age, or one related to the particular characteristics of liquid in glasses. Therefore children were also given rectangles of varying sizes on which they had to made area judgments. Again, eleven-year-olds employed a height-times-width rule, conforming to the mathematically correct model for area assessment. Five-year-olds, however, did not perform as they had with liquids (using height alone to judge size). They used width as well as height, but in an unexpected fashion. The five-year-olds appeared to employ a height-*plus*-width rather than a height-times-width rule.[2]

Because the height-alone judgment did not occur with rectangles (or in a later study with triangles), Anderson and Cuneo suspected that the five-year-olds' disregard for width in estimating liquid quantity might be a function not of limitations on encoding capacity (that is, of centration) but of highly learned habits stemming from everyday experiences with drinking and judging liquid quantity in glasses. In this everyday situation, where the glasses a child encounters are typically of a standard size, the height of the liquid is the most important cue in judging the amount to drink. When one drinks, the height of liquid changes as the amount left diminishes, making height highly salient.

Further tests with quantity judgments appeared to support this type of interpretation. When five-year-olds were given wax cylinders to judge, their quantity estimates varied depending on whether or not the wax was presented inside a beaker. With wax inside a beaker, a height-only model was used; but when the wax was presented without a beaker, a height-plus-width model was employed.

Thus, the results of this series of experiments suggest some interesting conclusions. Anderson and Cuneo claim that they have obtained the first unambiguous support for the widely held conviction that the nonconserving child focuses on only one dimension, height, in judging liquid quantity. However, this centration effect is apparently quite specific to the judgment of quantity within glasslike containers. When cylindrical volume is judged outside a container or when the area of a rectangular or triangular figure is judged, the young child incorporates information about both dimensions in judging area. But he appears to integrate cues from the two dimensions in an unexpected and nonoptimal fashion: an increase in width has the same magnitude of effect on quantity judgment for figures of different heights. For example, a 4×4 inch rectangle is judged to be just as much larger than a 4×2 inch one as an 8×4 inch rectangle is larger than an 8×2 inch one. The presence of a mature height-by-width model for estimation was not demonstrated for a majority of subjects until the surprisingly late age of eleven.

Anderson's argument that quantitative rather than merely qualitative performance models are necessary to untangle the roles of multiple determinants of performance can be illustrated by his rationale for rejecting the suggestion that he could have simply compared subjects' area estimates for two carefully chosen figures in order to determine their models for judging quantity. More specifically, the suggestion was made that by comparing performance on two rectangles, one measuring 4 × 14 inches and one measuring 8 × 8 inches, one would have a critical test of whether a subject uses an additive or a multiplicative model. A simple additive rule would yield larger area estimates for the first rectangle (18 versus 16 square inches) while a simple multiplicative rule finds the second figure to be larger (56 versus 64 inches). However, as Anderson points out, this comparison can be used to reveal what rule a subject is using only if one assumes: (1) that height and width are subjectively measured on the same scale; (2) that this subjective scale is linearly related to actual length; and (3) that the subject using an additive rule weighs height and width equally in making subjective estimates of area (see Anderson and Cuneo, p. 353, n. 1). To illustrate the point, if the young child estimates area by an additive model but assigns twice as much weight to height as to width, his subjective assessment of each rectangle corresponds to a weighted sum — 2(4) + 14 = 22, versus 2(8) + 8 = 24 — and he will judge the second rectangle to be larger just as the child who uses a multiplicative rule does. Thus, an analysis of the size of area estimates for different problems rather than a qualitative comparison is called for.

The functional measurement technique is a variant of the mathematical model approach, but it has two distinguishing characteristics: it is particularly suited for studying certain types of cognitive behavior (ratings, attitudes, or judgments involving the integration of multiple factors); and it yields a validated response scale. This second feature (which has not been stressed so far) is of considerable importance because it is useful in justifying the interpretation of statistical interactions between group and treatment variables. (See the appendix for a discussion of the interpretation of interactions and the problems related to uncertainties about the response scale.)

The functional measurement approach has been slow to gain acceptance in comparative cognitive research, perhaps because the techniques grew out of the technical area of measurement theory and psychophysics. But Anderson has shown in his recent publications that it is a powerful technique for describing cognitive activity in a wide range of areas relevant to this enterprise. (For other extensions of functional measurement analysis see Anderson, 1980.)

Advantages of Model-based Research Strategies

Model-based research is a logical extension of the general strategy of applying task analysis to comparative cognitive research; but models represent more detailed and explicit analyses than the verbal formulations that psychologists conventionally apply to the tasks they use. In developing and testing task models, the researcher forces himself to confront squarely the fact that cognitive tasks involve multiple components. Our ability to specify how a difference in one processing component (whether a result of development, education, or physiological differences) will affect group differences in performance of the task is seriously restricted unless we have a theory that explicitly incorporates all of the necessary aspects of that task. A provocative article by Richard Bogartz (1976) illustrates the way in which developing a precise task model makes the researcher's assumptions explicit and permits stronger inferences about group differences. Bogartz reexamined the results of a study of developmental differences in distractibility conducted by Hale and Stevenson (1974). In the original study, five- and eight-year-old children were required to remember the locations of sequentially presented items. This task was administered under two conditions, one of which was designed to distract the subjects and one of which provided no distraction. Following the usual experimental logic, the researchers had reasoned (as would most psychologists) that if five-year-olds are more susceptible to distraction than older children, the difference in performance under the two distraction conditions would be larger for them than for eight-year-olds. Hale and Stevenson found that the difference between the distraction and no distraction conditions was not larger for five-year-olds than for eight-year-olds, and they concluded that they had found no support for the hypothesis that distractibility decreases with age.

Bogartz argues that such a conclusion is not justified. In order to interpret a comparison of performance differences for two groups in terms of process differences, one has to have an explicit model of the way in which the process of interest fits in with the other processes involved in performing the task. Bogartz developed a model for Hale and Stevenson's memory task, in which distractibility was measured in proportional terms. The model included the following assumptions and parameters.

1. Each time he is called upon to respond, a subject remembers the correct location of the target item with some probability, p.

2. If the subject does not remember the correct location (which will happen with probability $1 - p$) he guesses, and his guess is correct with some probability, g.

3. Distracting conditions will reduce the probability that the subject will remember the correct location for the item. That reduction can be represented as a lowering of p to rp, where r is a value between 0 and 1 and represents the subject's resistance to distraction. (Thus the higher r is, the higher is the probability of remembering the correct location under distracting conditions.)

4. The probability of remembering the correct item location increases with age. Using subscripts to denote age, we can formalize this assumption as: $p_8 \quad p_5$.

5. The research hypothesis is that distractibility decreases with age, or inversely, that resistance to distraction increases ($r_8 \quad r_5$). The null hypothesis is that distractibility does not differ for the two age groups ($r_8 = r_5$).

The probability of observing a correct response can now be specified for each cell in the original experimental design. For example, in the No Distraction condition (ND), the probability of a correct response for five-year-olds ($c_{5_{ND}}$) is equal to the probability that they remember the correct location (p_5) plus the product of the probability of a correct guess (g) times the probability that they do not remember the location ($1 - p_5$):

$$c_{5_{ND}} = p_5 + (1 - p_5)g.$$

Similarly, for the eight-year-olds:

$$c_{8_{ND}} = p_8 + (1 - p_8)g.$$

The effect of the Distraction condition (D) is simply to reduce the probabilities for remembering the correct locations from p_5 to $r_5 p_5$ and from p_8 to $r_8 p_8$, giving:

$$c_{5_D} = r_5 p_5 + (1 - r_5 p_5)g$$

$$c_{8_D} = r_8 p_8 + (1 - r_8 p_8)g.$$

These formulas permit us to express algebraically the effect (I) in which we are interested—the Group × Task interaction (the difference between performances in the No Distraction and Distraction conditions for the eight-year-olds minus the difference between performances for the same set of conditions for the five-year-olds):

$$
\begin{aligned}
I = {} & (c_{8_{ND}} - c_{8_D}) - (c_{5_{ND}} - c_{5_D}) \\
= {} & [p_8 + (1 - p_8)g] - [r_8 p_8 + [1 - r_8 p_8)g] - \\
& \{[p_5 + (1 - p_5)g] - [r_5 p_5 + (1 - r_5 p_5)g]\}.
\end{aligned}
$$

This equation reduces to:

$$I = (1 - g) [(1 - r_8)p_8 - (1 - r_5)p_5].$$

In the case where the null hypothesis holds and $r_8 = r_5 = r$, the equation reduces to:

$$I = (1 - g) (1 - r) (p_8 - p_5).$$

Under the null hypothesis, I can be zero (indicating there is no interaction in the data) only if one of the three terms in this equation is zero. Because we have assumed that the probability of correctly remembering a location is greater for the older children, p_8 is greater than p_5, and $p_8 - p_5$ cannot equal zero. The term $1 - g$ could be zero only if g were equal to 1, meaning that all guesses were correct and that performance was perfect. Similarly, $1 - r$ could be zero only in the case where r equals 1, meaning that there is no effect of distraction. Assuming that these latter two conditions do not hold (as was the case in Hale and Stevenson's data), there is no way to obtain a zero interaction under the null hypothesis. Under Bogartz's model, the failure to find a difference in the magnitude of the distraction effect at the two age levels supports the research hypothesis of age differences in distractibility, not the null hypothesis as in Hale and Stevenson's interpretation. From a commonsense viewpoint, this relationship is explained by the fact that Bogartz's model is one of proportional change in memory as a result of distraction. When distractibility is equal at the two ages (r_8 equals r_5), the difference between p and rp will be greater, the greater p is. Thus, if the probability of remembering the correct location is greater for the eight-year-olds ($p_8 > p_5$), the same susceptibility to distraction would result in a *larger* difference between performances in the No Distraction and Distraction conditions for them than for the five-year-olds. What the presence or absence of a Group × Task interaction means, therefore, is contingent upon the particular performance model the researcher chooses.

Thus, when dealing with a task involving several component processes, the presence or absence of group differences in the degree to which some manipulation affects task performance is interpretable only with reference to a specific theoretical model. Many researchers do not develop full-scale performance models, and such models may not be necessary if the task has been well analyzed and all the assumptions and parameters involved in the experimental design are clear. The problem is that most of us do not formally elucidate all the assumptions involved in our studies, and often we are not even aware of some of the assumptions we are making. When we interpret a test for a Group × Task interaction in performance data, we are in effect accepting certain assumptions about the nature of the interrelationships among variables. Hale and Stevenson's logic, for example, contained the assumption that the impact on performance of a given degree of distractibility would be the same at different overall performance levels. This assumption may or may not be correct (and Hale and Stevenson may or may not have wanted to make it); but until it is empirically tested, the interpretation of interactions between distraction conditions and groups that vary in performance level is ambiguous.[3] One of the chief benefits of the model-based research approaches is the requirement they impose on the researcher to be explicit about assumptions concerning the factors that are involved in performance and the ways in which these factors combine to produce the observed responses. Once such assumptions are out in the open, they can be evaluated for psychological plausibility or put to empirical test. When the assumptions concerning the (possibly multiple) causes underlying test performance are not explicit, Group × Task interactions may mislead the researcher about the foundations for her process-related inferences.

Because of these qualities of specificity and explicitness, model-based approaches have considerable potential for helping us understand the nature of cognitive performance in different kinds of subjects and for providing a rational basis for instruction. A detailed analysis of the subject's problem-solving rules at various ages appears more likely than do measures of performance accuracy at different ages to show us what it is about the child's understanding that is changing with age. A comparison of the components of mature and immature task performance models may suggest the points in performance at which problems might arise for the less proficient learner. In addition, being able to diagnose the individual's current level (what rule he is using or what processes he employs) should tell us what things we must teach him if we are to instill more proficient performance. Finally, we have a reasonable standard for evaluating the effects of training or instruction. Rather than just saying that the child makes a greater number of accurate predictions on balance-scale problems, for example, we can assess how far his knowledge of how to solve these problems has advanced in reference to both its initial state and to the ultimate goal of the adult's formal problem solution.

Cautionary Notes

These formal methods for describing psychological tasks and the behaviors they elicit represent some of the most powerful tools of analysis available to cognitive psychology. At the same time, however, the methods are subject to some potential liabilities. These dangers are by no means unique to formal analysis, but they are brought into sharp relief by the very precision that formal analysis introduces into comparative cognitive research.

Perhaps the greatest pitfall in all experimental work about thinking processes arises from a confusion between what we think the task entails and what subjects who enter these tasks actually deal with in their efforts to comply with the demands placed on them. This problem has come up over and over again as we have reviewed the many ways in which the task-as-analyzed may differ from the task-as-received by the subjects in our experiments.

Task specification is recognized as a serious issue in standard cognitive research. It is dealt with first of all by attempts to make the instructions convey exactly what the subject is to do, by introducing various constraints on what he is allowed to do, and by conducting pilot studies to assure oneself that the task is indeed what it is asserted to be. Despite these precautions, before experimenters can specify the task with any degree of certainty they often have to resort to a series of studies in which conditions for behaving become more and more carefully constrained and unwanted behaviors are gradually eliminated.

This well-accepted iterative procedure for producing valid task analyses results in side effects that cannot be ignored in comparative cognitive research. For one thing, it is usually assumed that "the task" is a bounded set of environmental contingencies, distinct and separate from the social circumstances in which they are embedded. From this point of view, it doesn't matter if instructions are given by a person or a tape recorder; the stimuli may be presented on 3 x 5 cards or a computer display screen; the responses may be noted down on a scrap of paper or may consist of key strokes on a computer consol.

Sometimes, of course, this assumption about the task is recognized as incorrect, and in rare circumstances it has been made the object of study (for example, in studies of how experimenter expectations affect behavior). By and large, however, the tasks that are used to study cognition (and hence, the tasks used in comparative cognitive research) can be presented by computer; they involve manipulation of symbols in a potentially self-contained system.

At other times it is incorrect to assume that *the* cognitive task is independent of the context in which it is presented. Yet that error often goes undetected. Moreover, the assumption of such independence means that possibly relevant background factors are difficult to think about because they are not part of our models. Many such characteristics of experimental cognitive tasks are well known to us from our own school experience even if we have not been subjects in an experiment. When we engage in a cognitive task, we know that in some sense we are being tested; as often as not, we think that some aspect of our intelligence is at issue. Special rules apply to such situations, although we cannot be certain about all of them. We know better than to ask how to carry out the task successfully — the experimenter is not likely to give us the answer. We also know (or we are soon told) that it is not permissible to jot down notes, to dawdle, or to change our minds. Even so, a lot of what happens to us is very difficult to interpret in terms of our past experience with cognitive tasks; failure to "psych out" the problem is not uncommon.

So long as such puzzlements are common to *all* subject groups in an experiment their existence need not be disabling; they will constitute underspecification of the factors that control behavior. They will simply put unexplainable (error) variance into the results.

But in comparative cognitive research, we face the real danger that such background factors will be differentially influential for different groups. When this happens, the error variance is *not* randomly distributed. Insofar as one group of subjects responds to features of the task environment that are inappropriate to the solution of the task, this nonrandomness will operate to depress the performance of that group. In short, such groups will appear to suffer a cognitive deficit.

Time and again in the studies we have reviewed, the possibility or the demonstrated actuality of such faulty analyses has appeared. It is referred to directly by Goodnow in her comment that non-Western, nonschooled children come to experiments with expectations about appropriate behavior that are inappropriate to the test situation. The same difficulty comes up when we discover that instructions given in mundane language "understandable by anyone" are not understood in equivalent ways by different subjects. Although not usually thought of in this way, the same issue is implicated when we worry about some of our subjects being frightened, or easily distracted, or unmotivated. In all such cases, background features of the task are not neutral. In these and many other situations, we need to realize that the task our subjects work on may be different from what our analysis allows. This is important because a side effect of the assumption that cognitive tasks are independent of the context within which they are presented is the temptation to believe that once a task has been designed and specified in logically complete detail, the same task can be given to different populations with the assurance that it will, in fact, be the same.

Within a formal modeling framework this assumption is especially attractive, so attractive that it may slow recognition of circumstances when it ought to be abandoned. Each of the models we have discussed required a good deal of ingenuity and time, not to mention technical expertise and expense, to develop and test. If forced to conclude that groups being compared are responding to different task environments, the modeler's work would be doubled at least. It is within this framework that it is very tempting to attribute all performance differences to different values of the model's parameters (rate of forgetting, for example). It is much easier to adjust a model's parameters to fit a group's data than to consider the alternative that the difference may be attributable to the fact that different groups are working on different problems. In such cases, a *qualitative* difference in what the subjects are doing will be mistaken for a *quantitative* difference in what they are doing. This error is in no way specific to formal models, but those who employ formal models are particularly tempted to make it because the counterassumption so greatly complicates their already difficult task.

A response pattern noted by Baylor and Gascon in their work on seriation of weight illustrates these difficulties. During their experiment one Stage 1 child said that the last block presented to her was the heaviest. She had placed it on the balance beam by itself and explained: "It was the last; it was all alone; it's that one . . . then I weighed the others and they are medium heavy, and it's heaviest" (p. 17). Since the child had placed the chosen block in the scale pan with no comparison block on the other side of the balance beam, the block plummeted to the table. Judging from her explanation, Baylor and Gascon guessed that the speed with which the pan dropped was the critical stimulus factor for this subject. Nowhere in their model is there provision for this possibility; therefore, insofar as their guess is correct, their model must be in error.

A similar difficulty arose from contextual factors when Resnick and Glaser (1976) tried to teach children to carry. When children trained to assign numerals to columns of fewer than ten blocks were given columns with more than ten, some looked up at the experimenter, rather than at the stimulus items in front of them, for a solution to the problem. The children then had to be taught, as a part of the training, that the experimenter was not a relevant aspect of the problem.

A final note of caution about formal task analyses and models should be aimed at the assumption of a static task environment within which a single set of behaviors can be found. The reason for assuming that a task remains the same for an individual all the time he is dealing with it is obvious; if the task changed in the middle of an experiment, the analysis would have to change accordingly and the analytic problems would be greatly compounded. Convenience notwithstanding, there is ample reason to believe that tasks, as they are worked on by living subjects, do change even in the course of a single experimental session and that people can be found responding in different ways at different times within a single problem.

This observation follows more or less directly from the fact that experience with an experimental task can change a subject's ideas of what behaviors are required as well as her skill in carrying out required behaviors. Battig (1975) laments the difficulty of achieving a detailed model of adult verbal learning because he found not only that individual subjects differed from one another in the remembering strategies they used, but that most subjects seemed to employ different strategies at different times within what he considered a single task environment. Our earlier work on children's concept learning (Cole, 1976) convinced us that young children faced with learning difficulties may greatly broaden the set of environmental aspects they incorporate into their problem-solving activity (looking even to the position of the experimenter's hands or inadvertent smudges on pictures for clues). They also change the kinds of learning strategies they employ, sometimes searching actively for a rule to encompass all aspects of the problem, sometimes attempting to remember specific correct answers, sometimes giving in to despair and adopting a simple motor routine such as choosing stimuli on the left side on every trial.

The most blatant example of subject-controlled changes in cognitive activity in our experience occurred in a free recall experiment. A bright undergraduate quickly learned a list of twenty-four nouns divisible into four categories of six items each. After two presentations of the list, the entire set was recalled in perfect, categorically organized sets. On the third presentation all items were again recalled, but this time one item from each category was named before another item from that category was named — perfect "nonclustering." To complete the demonstration, this subject recalled the items in perfectly clustered fashion on the last trial of a five-trial experiment.

Such examples can be treated as amusing illustrations of the power of individuals to control their cognitive activity in ways not envisioned by our experimental techniques. Less amusing is the fact that such activity goes on in a variety of less easily detected ways, obscuring our analyses and rendering invalid our attempts at a theoretically valid specification of group differences in cognitive activity.

There are other difficulties in applying formal models to comparative cognitive research that could and should be considered by anyone who undertakes research in this area. Models simplify and often oversimplify. In order to implement models, we may create situations that artificially constrain people to behave as if their behavior followed the model's prescriptions when it does not. And so on. In our opinion, formal models are no more (or less) than the analytic tools that are a part of the general tool kit of science; and these tools alone cannot resolve the difficulties that this book is addressing.

6.

From Laboratory to Life

One reason for writing this book has been our growing concern about the sweeping generalizations that are often drawn from inconclusive comparative research. We realize that policy-oriented conclusions and recommendations will continue, not only because of a demand for scientific accountability but also because there is a need to improve the education of the young, the care of the mentally ill, and the skills of the economically disadvantaged, *now* even if the needed research has not been completed. But broad-ranging conclusions and recommendations have become commonplace, not just to the extent they are called for in setting policy or designing services, but also in academic journals, where they gain admittance under the shielding rubric of "discussion." Researchers usually know when they are going far beyond their data (except, of course, when their designs and procedures mislead them concerning that data). Speculation occurs so frequently and generalizations are repeated so often, however, that it is easy to believe that the generalizations have a basis in fact.

Of greatest concern to us is the frequency with which the poor performance of a special group on some experimental task is taken as evidence that its members lack a specific ability or process: not just that they do not show it in performing *that* task under *those* circumstances but that they lack it completely. This "finding" then becomes the basis either for restricting our aspirations for the group (for example, "preoperational children can't be taught science") or for focusing our attention almost exclusively on the presumed deficit ("poor children lack conceptual abilities and need to be taught to talk") when there may not be any such general inability. One basic means of avoiding this kind of erroneous overgeneralization—which may ultimately prove not just embarrassing to the social scientist but, more important, detrimental to the interests of the group in question—is the careful design of comparative cognitive research to ensure that group differences are related to process differences and that processing differences are explicitly interpreted within the context of specific tasks. If we sometimes have to extend ourselves beyond the research data to make practical recommendations in areas we have not directly studied, let us acknowledge that we are doing so and be sure that our data base is reasonably well built. Of course, for the researcher who is concerned about making treatment recommendations, good research design is a necessary but not a sufficient tool. The researcher with strong applied interests will be concerned that *diagnosis* using carefully constructed experimental contexts as analytic devices does not constitute *treatment*.

The kinds of strategies we have discussed may lead to a better understanding of the differences between groups in terms of processes activated within an experimental task, and additional, well-focused research may provide training or compensation for less proficient populations so that they perform more effectively *on the task in question*. However, the goal of the social program that provides the funding for applied social science research is to improve the *general* intellectual functioning of such groups as the "disadvantaged," "mentally ill," "developmentally delayed," or "learning disabled." An extensive training program that successfully improves the serial recall performance of persons in one of these categories would fall far short of satisfying this general aim unless there was some evidence that the trained processing skills are implicated in the group's difficulties in a range of everyday tasks. We would also want our training to produce improvement in performance of these everyday tasks. The current usefulness of process-based comparative research in meeting practical goals, then, is largely dependent upon two assumptions: (1) that the processing deficit uncovered within the context of a particular cognitive task is one that appears also in logically related real-life tasks of practical importance; and (2) that training the improficient to engage in appropriate cognitive activity in one task will lead them to use the same skill in the wider range of tasks in which it can be profitably employed. Easy acceptance of these assumptions, neither of which has a firm empirical basis in the kinds of cognitive tasks discussed in this book, is likely to lead sooner or later to disappointment.[1]

Easy acceptance of the first assumption is unwise in view of the possibility that laboratory tasks require strategies or abilities that are not crucial in many everyday activities, and also because a strategy that subjects fail to use in an experimental task may be one they do employ in natural situations where the task has some practical importance. The comparative research literature is replete with instances where the language, conceptual, or memory skills presumed lacking on the basis of laboratory experiments appear to be manifested in everyday activities. An incident reported by Farnham-Diggory (1972) illustrates the problem:

One researcher was recently heard to explain the importance of a double classification principle to a group of social scientists. He presented a curriculum to teach the principle to disadvantaged children, on the assumption that such a curriculum would increase their operational thinking. Listening to this presentation was a skeptical anthropologist, who insisted that the disadvantaged children in question already knew how to perform double classifications. "No," answered the psychologist: "My test results — using colors and shapes — prove that they don't. The average disadvantaged child in my sample couldn't correctly classify red diamonds, blue diamonds, red squares, blue squares, and materials of that sort." The anthropologist shrugged. "I don't know about your squares and diamonds," he said, "but any ghetto child knows that black is good, and policemen are bad, and that when he meets a black policeman he has a problem. *That's* a double classification." (pp. 37-38)

Is classifying a man as both black and a policeman the same as classifying an object as both red and square? We shouldn't be too quick to offer an answer to this type of question. To answer reasonably, we first have to analyze real-world cognitive activities in the same way that we analyze intellectual functioning within particular experimental tasks. This need brings us back to the requirement that we *verify* the hypothesis that the processes studied and trained in the laboratory are of some practical importance in everyday life. Unfortunately, this demand is not an easy one to satisfy.

Comparing Laboratory and Real-Life Tasks

Anyone engaged in applied comparative cognitive research must take very seriously the problem of establishing that the process differences that are the focus of most laboratory research will play a significant role in the nonlaboratory environments where subjects turn back into people. This is a difficult problem for two reasons. First, it is by no means clear how to find out what is going on in particular nonlaboratory environments in order to assess the relevance of the information discovered in the laboratory. Second, there is substantial reason to believe that even when a case for potential relevance can be made, the conditions for thinking outside the laboratory may render the specialized behavior irrelevant in practice.

Consider for a moment the skeleton of the procedures upon which laboratory inferences rest. The researcher invents a task that has two or more variants. These variants are designed to reveal a crucial difference in behavior that will permit the researcher to assert that, in the class of tasks encompassing the variants, "process P" is at work. The previous chapters have considered a variety of special difficulties that application of these procedures entails for comparative cognitive inferences. Most of these special cases boil down to the central difficulty of assuring that the task as we propose it in our experiment is the task that all subjects are actually responding to. When we err in this central aspect of our experiment, our attribution of group differences to process P goes awry; statements about cognitive process are, at base, theoretical statements about the relationships between task environments (stimuli) and behaviors; if our specification of the task is incorrect, our process claims become moot.

We have already described (in chapter 3) Blank's (1975) test of the popular hypothesis that young children fail to evoke appropriate verbal labels when learning a discrimination. She demonstrated that the question "Why did you choose that block?" was not the same stimulus for little children as for adults. The children in such studies are responding to a different set of stimulus conditions *from their point of view*, disabling these tasks as indicators of "verbalization ability" or any other single process separating children from adults. Similar remarks apply to almost every piece of research we have reviewed. Within the context of experimentation, we have strongly emphasized the care that must be taken (usually via a series of closely related experiments supplemented by explicit models wherever possible) to establish comparative inferences about process.

If we encounter so much difficulty in task specification within the confines of the laboratory, where we have a good deal of control over the environment and can use all of our accumulated knowledge as psychologists to render plausible our description of the task, consider the difficulties we face when we study cognitive behavior in real-life situations. There we must give up the power to design environments to our own specifications, and there subjects have many more options in selecting strategies for solving a given problem. If someone needs to remember a list of things, he can reach for a pencil and write them down. Alternatively, a person headed for the market, instead of writing down what he needs, may wander up and down the aisles, letting the well-organized market displays "remember" for him. A recalcitrant problem may simply go away of its own accord (a feature of life that every bureaucrat comes to count on), and in environments where other people are involved, one may get help with part or all of the task that concerns him.

As adults we know a great deal about how to get as much done with as little effort as possible in our everyday thinking. What little study has been done on children's knowledge of how to use their minds in everyday situations suggests that they are by no means naive in this regard and that their repertoire of skills includes a good deal that is *not* represented in any of the experiments described here. After interviewing children concerning their knowledge about remembering, Kreutzer, Leonard, and Flavell (1975) report on children's tendency to rely on other people to help them remember in everyday situations:

The use of this resource requires still less in the way of school-taught representational skills, trades on a well-learned set of social help-seeking routines, and — shades of Luria — would be most unlikely to turn up as an observed "mnemonic strategy" in a conventional laboratory study of memory development. Other people are in fact remarkably useful "amplifiers" of our storage and retrieval capacities. They can help you prepare for future retrieval by guiding your learning strategy or otherwise assisting study, by storing part of all of the information themselves, or by helping you commit it to a reliable store external to both of your heads. Similarly, they can aid retrieval by helping you select and execute internal or external search strategies, by actively joining in the search themselves, by letting you know if they should chance to recall or encounter the lost item later, or by recruiting others to similar active or passive helping roles. The younger children in this study seemed to be aware of at least a few of these possible forms of mnemonic assistance by others.   (pp. 51-52)

Great flexibility in using whatever device is at hand stands out as an important characteristic of everyday remembering, but another element of remembering in natural situations is important also. Remembering is something one does in order to do something else; it is not the goal of activity. This "instrumental" characteristic of cognition in which the goals of behavior are closely related to the means was emphasized early on by Vygotsky (1978) as a principal distinction between laboratory and everyday contexts of cognition. Istomina's work (1975), based directly on these ideas, demonstrates that embedding a cognitive task (in her case, free recall) in a context where the goal of remembering is clear and meaningful as part of an understood social role greatly changes the nature of young children's remembering activities.

Istomina pointed out that in a certain sense there can be no doubt that three- and four-year-old children understand what remembering means. They not only use remembering-type words in their everyday vocabulary in a way that is grammatically appropriate and obviously instrumental ("Remember, mommy, you promised to buy me a doll"), but they can also display exceptional ability in remembering aspects of prior events that adults have difficulty recalling. However, three- and four-year-old children are very unlikely to understand remembering as an objective toward which their activity must be channeled. Rather, remembering activity is almost always a means to some other goal.

When three- and four-year-olds are faced with a typical

laboratory task (Istomina used a free recall task in which the objects to be remembered were displayed on a table), their goals are likely to center on maintaining interaction with the adult. In such a situation, remembering is not intrinsically related to the motives of the child's behavior, but is interjected into the social interaction by the adult in a way that requires the child to create within himself the needed motives and activity.

However, if remembering is made a means of fulfilling goals that the child has adopted, the activity of remembering is clearly related to his overall goals, and by implementing the overall goals, remembering will get done too.

To demonstrate this contrast and its consequences, Istomina compared her standard free recall task to a free recall task using exactly the same items within a social situation — playing kindergarten with needed supplies from a play grocery store. Each child had a clearly defined role in this activity that occurred repeatedly. The recall task arose whenever a child was given the role of "purchasing agent" for the kindergarten on a particular day. In that case, the child was given the free recall task as an oral shopping list that had to be remembered and repeated when she went to the make-believe market.

Central to our concerns is Istomina's demonstration of a qualitative difference in children's behavior in the two settings, with the specific nature and degree of the difference depending upon the age of the child. For the very youngest children (three-year-olds), the nature of remembering as a deliberate activity was obscure. Embedding the recall task in a social situation was of little help because the children did not attempt to transmit the required message and therefore no remembering was evident. With slightly older children (four-year-olds), the social setting provided by the role-play was enough to get them to try to transmit the message and to realize that specific remembering activity is necessary, although they were not especially skillful in what they did to remember. Still older children engaged in sophisticated remembering activities when playing the grocery store game but not when simply told to remember items as part of a standard recall task. For the oldest children (six- and seven-year-olds), the play situation made no real difference to recall. They appeared to recognize remembering as a distinct kind of activity that can be called on in any situation.

Using normative procedures appropriate to the life of very young children, Istomina was able to create a model of a real-life situation under laboratory circumstances. Occasionally, situations can be found outside the laboratory that are "true to life" but still allow the investigator to specify the task fairly well. Neisser and Hupcey (1974) reported on an ingenious use of a naturally occurring memory "test" that allowed them to test some hypotheses about memory for information in lengthy stories. Their subjects were members of a club that met regularly to discuss the Sherlock Holmes stories. At these meetings, members would test one another on their ability to identify the source of a line or passage read out of context: for example, "What story first used the line 'Elementary, my dear Watson'?" and "From whom was the purloined letter taken?"

Neisser and Hupcey used this circumstance and other information that they collected from the members of the club (how long they had been reading Doyle's stories, how often they had read each story) to test hypotheses about the kinds of retrieval cues that are most effective for recall. Although the fact that subjects were interrogated singly in a laboratory setting rather than in the social surrounding of the club may have introduced some changes into the task, it seems reasonable to conclude that the club activities provided an unusually fine model setting in which to study the way people remember prose.

Neisser and Hupcey's demonstration suggests a whole range of contexts in which studies of cognition closely related to everyday life activity could be carried out. Telephone operators, air traffic controllers, waiters, shoemakers, and many other people engaged in specific job-related tasks must accomplish their work in a circumscribed setting that is constrained in various ways by the demands of the job. It may well be that a theoretically useful way to engage in work with some populations who have been the object of comparative cognitive research is to study their behavior in job settings. By combining diagnostic research and training, researchers might be able to provide target populations with useful skills even if the results of their theoretically oriented research are disappointing. (Singleton, 1977, presents many useful examples of settings where cognitive research can be combined with job-related activities.)

If we are to study cognitive functioning in real-life contexts, however, we have to deal with the fundamental difficulty of establishing that a particular task is "occurring" in the absence of experimental controls, or strong social-organizational rules that constrain people sufficiently to enable a plausible analysis.

The following transcript is taken from an article by Cole, Hood, and McDermott (1978, p. 57), who videotaped eight- and nine-year-old children participating in an after-school cooking club. As the transcript opens, Nadine and Dolores are partners, working through a recipe for cranberry bread.

1. Nadine:	(picks up the recipe and reads) ¾ a teaspoon of nut-nutmm-nutmeg.	
2. Dolores:	Here's the nutmeg (holds plastic bag with chopped walnuts).	
3. Nadine:	Here's the recipe.	
4. Nadine:	(gets recipe) Is that nutmeg? Let's just skip that.	
5. Dolores:	It's nuts.	
6. Nadine:	One cup of sugar. O.K. What do we need? (looks at recipe) ¾'s, ¾'s a teaspoon nutmeg. We have	

to, how do you sift this? (measures three ¼ tea-
spoons of the nuts and puts them in sifter)
(Dolores and Nadine "sift" the nuts)
7. Lucy: (coming over to table) Where's the flour?
8. Nadine: I don't know. This is bad. I don't think this is
                 working out right. How are you supposed to sift
                 nutmeg? (puts hand in sifter)
9. Rikki: (comes over) *You are*, Nadine. You're supposed to
                 sift it.
10. Nadine: Where's the nutmeg?
11. Rikki: Over on the table.
     (Nadine, Rikki, and Dolores go to other table)
12. Nadine: Where?
     (Rikki hands Nadine the nutmeg)

The first thing to notice is that the transcript is not easy to
follow. The problem isn't that it is too skimpy, although it
doesn't describe the room, the table full of cooking parapher-
nalia, the other children present and what they are doing, or
the physical positions of Dolores and Nadine. But "skimpiness"
is not the right word for the difficulty. If we added all of the
additional information that would be needed for the reader to
grasp readily the many features of the scene, we would need
pages of description that would be virtually unreadable.

This descriptive problem rarely arose in our discussion of experiments, and for an important reason: experiments are
designed to cut through the complexities of everyday life contexts for thinking and lay bare the "basic" process. Because we
do the designing, and so many features of experiments remain
invariant from one study to the next (at least in principle), we
feel that we know what is going on when we read a bare
description. Only when our predictions fail are we pushed to
take another look for missing details.

Keeping in mind this central difficulty of providing a *relevant* description, what kind of description can we offer of
Nadine and Dolores preparing cranberry bread? Clearly, problem solving is a group activity in this situation. Not only the

assigned "partners" but other children (Lucy and Rikki) are involved in this brief episode during the bread-baking activity. This example also demonstrates how the "task of the moment" fluctuates over time and is open to the possibility of modification. In line 1, Nadine's "task" appears to be locating ¾ of a teaspoon of nutmeg, which is a problem because nutmeg is an unknown quantity to her. Dolores offer a "solution" (albeit an incorrect one) to the problem in line 2, but Nadine appears to remain uncertain in line 4 and suggests that they modify their goal ("Let's just skip that") rather than immediately accepting Dolores's answer. Accordingly, Nadine goes on to the next ingredient in line 6 (one cup of sugar) but then returns to the nutmeg "task," perhaps in response to Dolores's insistence ("It's nuts"). In line 8 Nadine appears to address a new problem: the recipe says to sift the nutmeg and she doesn't know how to sift nuts. Alternatively, we might characterize Nadine as still working on the same problem (identifying nutmeg) since the unsuitability of walnuts for sifting supports her doubts about nutmeg being nuts. Whichever task description is more accurate, while Nadine is tackling this problem she is also engaged in another — responding to Lucy's question ("Where's the flour?"). Finally, the solution to the nutmeg problem is provided by Rikki, who was not one of the partners originally confronted by the task. Thus, even this very brief sequence of behavior illustrates that everyday cognitive tasks are difficult to isolate, fluctuate from moment to moment, are carried on in combination with other goals, and can be approached through different strategies, including the use of other people to assist (or hinder) in problem solution.

We would offer a solution to the analytic difficulties that such scenes present if we could, but at present there is no accepted method even for describing real-world scenes, let alone for specifying how cognitive activities go on in them. We can, however, assert that the problem is acute for anyone who wants to apply knowledge gained in well-specified laboratory tasks. We can also report on some strategies currently in use by cognitive psychologists who have had to face up to these complexities.

Training Cognitive Processes

One approach to this problem is to identify some process that you have reason to believe is generally important, and then train subjects in it in such a way as to maximize its utility. Among the researchers whose work we have discussed, this issue has received the most careful attention from Brown and Campione (1977, 1978) and Butterfield and Belmont (1977), two research teams working with the mentally retarded. As both teams have pointed out, researchers have been fairly successful in training retarded individuals to employ specific cognitive processes or strategies within specific tasks: Brown, Campione, Bray, and Wilcox's (1973) training of retardates to cumulatively rehearse in the keeping-track task (described in chapter 4) is one such example. However, there have been repeated failures when researchers have tested to see whether their subjects generalize trained strategies to new tasks. When Brown and her colleagues' subjects were retested six months after their original training in cumulative rehearsal, they still showed the positive effect of training on the keeping-track task (Brown, Campione, and Murphy, 1974). However, there was no apparent generalization of this strategy to a similar task that involved remembering a series of numbers.

This lack of generalization even to tasks that our analyses indicate are similar implies that producing general changes in the young, emotionally disturbed, learning disabled, or retarded will not be a simple matter. If subjects learn to rehearse in one particular task but do not generalize that training to other tasks where memory rehearsal is helpful, it would seem that they must be trained in a host of tasks if any general improvement in cognitive functioning is to be obtained. Considering the scope of the effort required to develop and confirm a model of task performance in any *one* task and to devise efficient training techniques for it, training subjects in every task of practical importance would be an undertaking of Herculean proportions, and if it did not ultimately prove useful to the person trained, a lot of effort would have been wasted. As Butterfield, Wambold, and Belmont (1973) have pointed out: "to induce general cognitive competence in retarded persons . . . would require systematic analyses of one cognitive domain after another, over a tremendous diversity of domains, with applied experiments along the way to show how to improve each component skill . . . The conglomerate enterprise would . . . be enormous, and its intermediate payoff unsure" (p. 668).

Some more recent formulations of the generalization issue have been more optimistic, however (Brown and Campione, 1977; Butterfield and Belmont, 1977; Brown, 1978). Brown and Campione (1978) argue that previous failures to find generalization of training for young, retarded, or unschooled subjects cannot be regarded as legitimate evidence that these subjects will not generalize learned processing skills to new situations, because the training has usually not been suitably designed to foster such a transfer. Brown and Campione provide a set of guidelines for formulating training in such a way that generalization will be promoted:

1. Subjects receiving training should be given some direct feedback about the effectiveness of the trained activity or strategy. They may not always realize that employing the strategy has improved their performance, in which case they have little incentive for maintaining it in a new task.

2. The subjects' training should take place in several different task contexts. (This undertaking can be implemented in concert with the next recommendation.)

3. Subjects should be given direct instruction about generalization. The experimenter can inform the subjects that the strategy would be useful in a number of different tasks and that when given a new task, they should decide whether it would prove facilitative. This last skill may be developed by providing both experience and explicit instructions with additional tasks on which the strategy would be appropriate, as well as on tasks for which it would not be appropriate.

In evaluating the failure of previous training programs to obtain generalization of training, then, two points should be remembered: first, that most of these programs fell short of Brown and Campione's guidelines; and second, that the knowledge and skills involved in executing a skill when trained to apply it are not identical to those entailed in deciding when to apply the routine in a new situation. We should not expect training aimed at the first type of change to necessarily produce the second type.

This argument leads to the notion that generalization is itself a skill that we can try to train. Recently, in fact, generalization has been treated as one skill belonging to a class of general problem-solving strategies that psychologists should attempt to teach. Among this class of general skills may be included such activities as planning, asking questions, checking one's answer for reasonableness, self-testing, and monitoring of ongoing activities (Brown and DeLoache, 1978). The rationale behind this viewpoint is that because these strategies are applicable across a wide range of tasks, training in their use will produce more general improvement in cognitive functioning than will training in task-specific strategies. Although the argument is reasonable, as yet there is little evidence that these theoretically general skills, once trained, will in fact be used in the range of tasks to which they are applicable. An exception, however, is a study by Brown and Barclay (1976), in which retardates were trained to test themselves in order to assess whether they were ready to be tested formally by the experimenter. The skill was originally taught within the context of a recall task. Two groups of subjects were trained to use a self-testing strategy (either trying to anticipate the next word on the study list before they looked at it or cumulative rehearsal) during the subject-paced study period. Both types of self-testing training led to better performance both immediately after training and one year later. More impressively, subjects who had received self-testing training with the recall task displayed better performance on a self-paced reading comprehension task, in which students were instructed to study a story until they were sure they could remember its gist. Students previously trained to assess their own test readiness in the recall task spent more time studying the stories, were more likely to demonstrate overt study activities such as note taking or testing themselves out loud, and recalled more idea units, especially those relevant to the main idea of the stories.

An earlier example of successful training and generalization of cognitive skills has been reported by Olton and Crutchfield (1969). A self-teaching program designed to foster the use of such problem-solving skills as thinking of a variety of different explanations for an occurrence, evaluating the likelihood of hypothetical explanations, and noting discrepancies in a situation (Covington, Crutchfield, Davies, and Olton, 1974) was given to fifth-grade children. Students receiving the training evidenced greater use of the measured thinking skills on new problems than did control group subjects, both immediately after training and six months later.

Although this research provides a foundation for optimism, that foundation is very thin. Efforts to devise training in such a way that a general skill will be effectively transferred to other tasks *not* included in the training process are likely to encounter major obstacles. The general skills that Brown and her colleagues advocate training may indeed be general, but they must be applied within specific tasks, and the particular characteristics of those tasks are likely to affect strongly the way in which the skill is applied (as well as the likelihood that the subject tries to apply it). Routinely applying a learned routine of "checking one's answer for reasonableness," for example, will be quite useless if the subject hasn't any idea what kinds of answers are reasonable in the new tasks.

Training Tasks of Practical Importance

Another approach to applying cognitive research is to select training tasks that are of considerable practical importance in themselves. Singleton's (1977) suggestions for studying job-related tasks exemplifies this approach. Other examples are found in the work of psychologists whose interest in educational relevance has led them to study such practically important tasks as counting, addition, finding geometric areas, and reading comprehension. In such cases, the skill being trained is important in everyday functioning, and hence, mastering it should significantly benefit subjects even if there is no transfer to other tasks. However, even though transfer to different *tasks* is not an issue here, transfer to different problem sets and other settings may still prove elusive, and this type of generalization is crucial if training is to have practical benefits. Brown and Campione's guidelines for training programs are equally important when this kind of generalization is at issue.

Thus, the generalization problem remains critical. It is difficult for the researcher to maintain confidence that processes such as cumulative rehearsal, vital to success in certain laboratory tasks, are of practical importance in real-life situations. We have argued that it is hard for psychologists to talk about and analyze real-life tasks in the same way that they analyze laboratory experiments. Although a solution to this problem is currently unavailable, the two lines of attack we have described (teaching either general problem-solving strategies or specific tasks of practical importance) offer hope of some degree of success. We have suggested that many educational and job-related tasks constitute promising areas for study since they have practical importance and yet appear tractable to experimental analysis and manipulation.

Additionally, the kind of task analysis required for training cognitive processes can be valuable in increasing our understanding of how these processes are applied and how they interact in different tasks. It may be just as well to abandon vague goals such as "improving cognitive competence" and concentrate instead on the specific processes and strategies used by "competent" thinkers.

It is important to note, though, that the strategies effective for "special" populations may not be identical to those employed by "normals" in performing the same tasks. For example, a five-year-old autistic child learning language does not face the same situation as a normal one-year-old at the same level of language development, and he may therefore not go about his task in the same way. These differences between special and normal populations contribute to practical problems and philosophical debates concerning the kinds of tasks that are appropriate for teaching special people, as well as how and where the teaching should be carried out.

Value Judgments in Cognitive Research

The importance of task context in cognitive performance coupled with the differences between laboratory tasks and real-world intellectual activity suggests the conclusion that the researcher concerned with producing practical improvement would do well to concentrate on studying cognitive processes within tasks that are as much like those important to subjects in everyday life as is practicable. In choosing a task for its practical importance, the researcher is going to have to make a value judgment about what skills are most important for his subjects to develop. There are basic social and ethical issues involved in such a selection process. When a researcher opts for studying language skills in the mentally retarded, concept formation in the deaf, or short-term memory in alcoholics, he is assuming that these things are not just present but are also important in the lives of individuals in the target group. This issue goes beyond the question of generalization, and touches upon the researcher's value system as he selects those skills he considers significant enough to warrant study and training.

In addition, the very act of comparing a special group with some other group of subjects designated as "standard" or "control" invites an implicit value judgment. The standard group's performance tends to take on an aura of "goodness." The use of one group's behavior as the standard of good performance is particularly questionable when the task elicits qualitative performance differences rather than some objectively measured degree of success. A word association task is perhaps the prime example of a task that produces *differences* in performance rather than varying degrees of success, but other examples from the cognition literature come readily to mind. Much comparative cognitive research has involved classification tasks, in which the subject is given a variety of items and instructed to place together those things that he thinks "go together." As in the word association task, subjects are often told explicitly that there are no right or wrong answers. However, the fact that young, non-Western, or elderly subjects tend to form types of groupings that differ from those of Western adults is then treated as evidence of a deficit (in abstract thinking or categorical organization of memory) in the special group under study. We need to remember that departures from the typical performance patterns of American adults are not necessarily deficits, but may indeed be excellent adaptations to the life circumstances of the people involved. Researchers must be cautious about placing values on certain types of performance simply because they are exhibited by their own reference group (see Goodnow, 1976). In the real world, placing sugar with flour (a categorical grouping typical of American adults in the laboratory task) will not always be more efficient than keeping the sugar near the coffee cups (a complementary grouping of the sort made by young, uneducated, or elderly subjects). Which type of classification is preferable will depend upon the context, that is, the number of different types of objects to be grouped and the way in which the materials are going to be used—in short, on the very aspects we take pains to eliminate from the experimental task. Since in the experimental task there is no knowledge available concerning how the items are to be used in the future, preference for one type of grouping over another is really no more than that—just a matter of preference. Training young children or persons from non-Western societies to classify as American adults do (and this has occurred) may serve no practical end. At the very least, the purpose should be spelled out, not assumed.

Until relatively recently, a similiar perspective on cognitive differences was prevalent in the research on nonstandard English dialects, especially Black English. The differences between those dialects and the textbook model of Standard English were presumed to be part of a syndrome of linguistic deprivation on the part of dialect users. Black English was considered an inferior vehicle both for the unambiguous expression of ideas and for conceptual thought per se (Deutsch, 1967; Bereiter and Engelmann, 1966). School districts and individual teachers endeavored to rid their pupils of nonstandard speech. In addition, a variety of language-based preschool programs were developed on the rationale that the differences embodied in Black English led to conceptual deficits that had to be overcome if children were to have a fair chance at later school success (Frost and Rowland, 1970). More recently, linguists' arguments that Black English is a dialect as serviceable as any other for expression and thought (see Labov, 1970), coupled with the repeated failure to causally connect the academic difficulties of some disadvantaged children with their use (or nonuse) of any particular language forms, has weakened the influence of this language deficit view. Nevertheless, the language deficit hypothesis has had considerable impact on the kind of education received by a great many children.

Another example of the role of value judgments is the controversy concerning what sorts of skills should be taught to the mildly (or educable in some taxonomies) retarded. In the past, the emphasis of intervention programs has been on teaching social and vocational skills (Taylor and Taylor, 1962). More recently, however, there has been a movement (now mandated by law) toward placing mildly retarded individuals within regular classrooms (mainstreaming), to give them more contact with nonretarded students and also more training in academic skills. Findings that mildly retarded individuals placed in regular classrooms tend to show higher levels of academic achievement than those placed in special classes (although it is generally questionable whether the placement caused the achievement difference) have provided ammunition for those arguing for mainstreaming. On the other side of the issue, some studies purport to show that special education classes do better in terms of promoting the retarded students' social skills and satisfaction with their own achievements. Baroff (1974) summarized the research on the pros and cons of special education placement in this manner, framing the issue in such a way that the basic question boiled down to a decision concerning what is most important for retarded individuals. Baroff's discussion of the placement issue shows how a social scientist's value judgments come into play when he attempts to summarize and draw implications from research findings.

> If it is agreed that the primary purpose of education is preparation for effective adulthood and that this should be the criterion for evaluating special education, the question of efficacy then becomes one of ascertaining how variations in class placement affect postschool adjustment . . . Is the quality of the postschool adjustment of retarded youth dependent on their academic status? At some level it must be, and yet retarded persons with reading and number skills that are virtually nonfunctional for activities of daily living somehow grossly manage to meet adult role expectancies . . . academic skills are relatively unimportant to vocational effectiveness in the unskilled jobs performed by most retarded individuals. While differences in academic achievement clearly affect employability in skilled as against unskilled jobs, *within* the range of unskilled employment its importance is lessened relative to the personality characteristics that employers of unskilled workers particularly value.   (pp. 250-251)

We do not wish to debate the merits of Baroff's assessment of the research and its implications; we are merely pointing out the extent to which his treatment reflects a value judgment.[2] His discussion clearly expresses the opinion that if, as his review of the research implies, there is a trade-off between social and vocational skills on the one hand and academic skills on the other, the former should receive priority in the education of the retarded. Two controversial and unexamined premises are at work here: (1) that the kinds of knowledge and conceptual skills generally labeled "academic" are relatively unimportant in daily nonwork activities and in unskilled occupations; and (2) that a position as an unskilled laborer is all that a mildly retarded individual should be trained for. The first premise bothers us on a theoretical level; despite the many differences between laboratory or school and "life," we reject the notion that the processes involved in academic skills are irrelevant to everyday activities. But the pragmatic consequences of such premises are more relevant to our point here. If the social ramifications of this viewpoint are not immediately obvious, they become so when one considers three facts: that placement in special education classes has often been based largely on IQ test performance; that an individual's IQ score may fluctuate as much as twenty points over time (quite enough to bring the individual out of the mildly retarded and into the normal or borderline-normal category); and that questions can be raised about the cultural fairness of these tests (the use of which typically results in the disproportionate assignment of minority students to special education programs). Viewed in this light, the potential social and human consequences of placing a higher value on social and (unskilled) vocational than on academic training for individuals diagnosed as mildly retarded should be clear.

An additional issue that the researcher interested in practical problems must face concerns *who* will receive his treatment. This issue becomes especially difficult when time and other resources are limited and the intervention is expected to benefit the subjects substantially. In some cases, the intervention will not be given to those who are thought not to need it, resulting in the loss of a control group for a simple treatment effect; at worst, however, subject selection can be strongly biased, posing a serious problem for interpretation of findings. Random assignment of eligible subjects is of course desirable whenever possible. However, ethical and organizational difficulties may sometimes result in selecting those who are "worst off" or those considered most likely to benefit from the treatment as subjects in the treatment group. When this occurs, investigators need to examine their results carefully for alternative explanations and to temper their conclusions appropriately if they find their samples to be biased. (See Cook and Campbell, 1976, and Campbell and Stanley, 1963, for discussions of how to proceed when this happens.)

On the Relevance of Basic Research

In the first chapter of this book we remarked upon the difficult position of the experimentally trained cognitive psychologist when he finds himself confronted by the need to "be relevant" in one of the many applied settings within which basic research increasingly is carried out.

While we believe that the strategies we have enumerated for dealing with these difficulties appear useful, it should be clear that we also view them as less than adequate for the work they are expected to accomplish.

This view emphatically does *not* imply that comparative cognitive research is useless and should be abandoned. In the discussions that led to the decision to produce this book, one of our colleagues remarked, "You're just telling people not to engage in bad research — what's the point of that?" To be sure, none of us wants to engage in research from which no important inferences can be drawn. But recognizing an error and being able to specify the actions needed to correct it are undertakings of vastly different magnitudes.

Our effort has been to identify those special threats to inference to which the comparative cognitive enterprise is especially vulnerable. It was obviously the strength provided by existing experimental and theoretical tools in modern experimental psychology that allowed us to analyze our weaknesses.

Our criticisms and suggestions should not be read as a condemnation of basic research, nor as a call to abandon accepted practices. Rather, we need a great deal more fundamental research that takes cognizance of the special problems we have been discussing.

We need more, not fewer, performance models and demonstrations of Group × Task interactions for tasks with better-specified task analyses.

We also need to consider combining such research with basic

research from other disciplines, such as sociology and anthropology, which are concerned with the description and analysis of the real-world settings where psychologists must apply their findings.

Complying with these suggestions is an enormous undertaking. But to pretend that it is easy—just a matter of running a few experiments or designing a summer training program—would be a self-deception that could only lead to disillusionment and failure. Only by recognizing the seriousness of these problems and trying to come to grips with them in our research strategies and theory building can we expect to improve our understanding of how people of different ages, cultures, or ability levels think.

Appendix. Statistical Issues in Comparative Research

While our primary emphasis has been on research design and interpretation, these concerns cannot be separated entirely from those of statistical analysis, and there are several quantitative issues that are particularly likely to arise when doing comparative research. Although we wanted to avoid a detailed technical treatment of measurement and statistics, this book would not be complete without some discussion of statistical questions involved in comparing groups of subjects that differ initially in terms of the variable being researched. In the discussion that follows, we will describe these issues from a commonsense viewpoint and will provide references for more complete, technical treatments in cases where an issue has received relatively little attention in basic texts on statistical methods for the social sciences.

Attempts to Control for Pre-existing Group Differences

One of the basic weaknesses of comparative research designs is the impossibility of obtaining comparison groups that are alike in all respects except one characteristic of interest. There is no simple solution to this problem, and hence relating group differences in performance to any single demographic characteristic is logically invalid. By advocating the use of a series of studies aimed at relating group differences to process differences, we have focused on the mechanisms (processes) that produce the dependent variables rather than on trying to prove that a particular causal independent variable is at work. But this strategy does not obviate our inability to relate group differences in a causal way to the particular demographic dimensions that are used to define comparison groups. There are, however, various procedures for equating comparison groups in terms of potentially confounding subject variables that are widely used in order to ameliorate this problem. We will briefly discuss these procedures even though their limitations have led us to avoid heavy reliance on them.

Matching on known characteristics

As mentioned in chapter 3, a procedure employed in many comparative investigations is to match subjects in terms of variables that are known to vary with group membership and are presumed to be important to the dependent measure. We stated then that matching subjects is not sufficient to solve the group equivalence problem because we can never be sure that we have matched on all relevant variables.

We illustrated this problem in chapter 3 with actual research on the susceptibility of different populations to the Muller-Lyer illusion. Some years ago, Underwood (1957) made the same point about the inefficacy of matching procedures.[1] In presenting a hypothetical example of a researcher trying to determine whether severity of schizophrenia is related to rigidity (difficulty in modifying habits), Underwood provides a convincing case for the inadequacy of matching.

We want the two groups to differ only on severity of schizophrenia . . . Suppose the two groups differed in age with the severe group having an older mean age. Suppose further that we actually knew that rigidity and age were positively related. If we find a difference in rigidity between our two schizophrenic groups, we would quickly realize that this could well be independent of the severity of schizophrenia. So, what do we do?

It would seem that we would have to turn to a matching procedure. So, we first match on chronological age. But this only? Well, no, perhaps we should match on sex, mental age, socio-economic background, racial background, education, length of stay in hospital, white blood count, weight, learning ability, number of siblings, and on and on. The point is that since we do not and cannot possibly know all the variables influencing rigidity and since we want all these variables equalized for the groups as long as they are not criteria used in diagnosis, we reach an impasse.   (pp. 116-117)

Besides being inadequate as a method of obtaining comparable groups, matching is a procedure that can create its own problems. Whenever matching on some variable requires selecting for comparison the extreme high scorers in one group and the extreme low scorers in another, the results are subject to certain artifacts of a statistical nature. Suppose we wanted to assess whether a program of directed viewing of Sesame Street was differentially beneficial in promoting "reading readiness" for black children from low-income homes as compared with white children from middle-income backgrounds. Before putting the children into our program of supervised viewing, we might be concerned that the two groups might differ initially in terms of reading-related skills such as knowledge of the alphabet and might decide that we should evaluate the effectiveness of the program for the two groups by looking at the posttreatment scores of subgroups from the two samples that are matched in terms of their prereading skills before entering the program. We could administer a reading-readiness test to all of the children who are going to receive our program of Sesame Street viewing and select subgroups of low- and middle-income children who are matched in terms of scores on the test. If the middle-income white children in our study had higher prereading scores on the whole than the low-income black children, we would have to select those children having the lowest scores in the middle-income sample to compare with those children having the highest scores in the low-income sample. The problem with this matching procedure is that it leads to an underestimation of the benefits of the program for the group that scores lower on the whole.

Any measurement involves a certain amount of error. Children receiving the lowest scores in a group will be those who are not only less skilled on the average than other members of their group but whose scores reflect a certain amount of negative measurement error as well. Similarly, the extreme high scores for a group will reflect a combination of superior ability and positive measurement error. In selecting matched subgroups for comparison, we are taking low-income children whose scores have large positive error components and middle-income children whose scores contain large negative error components. If we repeated the reading-readiness test before starting the Sesame Street viewing, the scores would not be exactly the same as on the first testing because the measurement error would have a different distribution. The result for the matched subgroups selected for comparison would be statistical regression toward the mean. Each subgroup would now have a mean score closer to the mean for their entire group (that is, the low-income subgroup would have lower scores on the average and the middle-income subgroup higher scores). What this effect means is that our subgroups were not really matched in terms of "true" prereading skills before the program started. If we were to compare scores obtained by these subgroups after directed viewing of Sesame Street, the comparison would be biased toward showing that middle-income children benefit more, because they had somewhat superior reading-related skills to begin with. Hence, matching can produce misleading results. The larger the initial difference between the comparison groups in terms of the characteristic or skill on which the matching is based (and the lower the correlation between the test or index used to measure that characteristic and the outcome measure), the larger this regression artifact is likely to be.[2]

Statistical matching: covariance techniques

Reseachers are currently more cognizant of the weaknesses of matching procedures such as those described above than they were at one time, and alternative methods are generally used to try to equate groups for potentially confounding differences. The Group × Task design can be considered in this context as an attempt to obtain groups equated in terms of performance on a control (compensatory) task by selecting a particular variant from the universe of possible tasks rather than by selecting atypical subgroups. (Some problems involved in this type of control for group differences will be discussed in the next section.) A procedure that is more directly comparable to matching is the use of statistical methods to "remove" the effects of potentially confounding subject variables. Instead of selecting matched subgroups for our Sesame Street study, we could analyze data from all children receiving the program but then use the pretreatment measure of their reading readiness as a covariate. Additional variables, such as the educational level of parents or the number of reading materials in the home, could be used as covariates as well. Theoretically, the analysis would indicate whether the reading-readiness scores the two groups of children receive after viewing Sesame Street would have differed if the subjects had been equivalent in terms of these covariates, that is, the relationship between income group and posttest score, with the effects of pretreatment reading readiness, parental education level, and reading materials in the home taken out. Using regression analysis, we could predict subjects' posttreatment scores on the basis of their pretreatment reading readiness, parental education, and reading materials in the home. The difference between predicted score and that actually obtained on the posttreatment test would then become the variable of interest, and we could test whether the size of this difference or "residual" score was different for the two income groups.

However, we are still confronted with the same problems that debilitate a matching procedure. First, any index used to measure a covariate, although related to the pretreatment differences between groups, would be unlikely to capture all of those differences. The problem of measurement error that arises when using pretest scores as a basis for matching occurs also in using demographic variables, such as parental education level, as covariates. Whatever index is used to measure parental education (perhaps years of formal school) will be an imperfect measure, unlikely to express the full extent of the educational differences between groups. For example, there will be not only inaccuracies in reporting years of education but also important differences between the two groups of parents in the quality of those years, resulting from differences in the types of schools attended and the programs undertaken. Second, there will be other, unmeasured differences between the groups of children as well. Just as we can never be sure that we have matched groups on all relevant variables, we can never be sure that we have used every important factor as a covariate. In this type of analysis, then, group differences prior to treatment again will be underestimated and in consequence the benefits that low-income black children derive from directed viewing of Sesame Street will be underestimated also.

Measuring differential gain scores

Another alternative would be evaluating the effects of the Sesame Street viewing program by comparing the two groups in terms of gain scores (the difference between reading-readiness posttest score and reading-readiness pretest score) rather than just posttest scores. But this tactic too has its drawbacks. Difference scores are less reliable than single-test scores, and this problem is particularly acute for gain scores (Mehren and Lehmann, 1980). In addition, differences in the reliabilities or difficulty values of two measures can produce artifactual Group × Task interactions (see the next section), and these problems are equally relevant when the two "tasks" are pretreatment and posttreatment tests of the same skills. Such artifactual results are quite common in the evaluation of programs administered to children over an extended period of time. Further, in the case of studies involving children, the picture is complicated by the fact that the children will be maturing during the period between the two testings and that a test's reliability and difficulty level typically vary with age. In general, the passage of time produces particular problems for interpretation of gain scores in comparative studies because we cannot specify what the growth curves are for different subject groups. A number of researchers have suggested that because learning is a cumulative process, those who have already reached higher levels will learn at a faster rate. Thus, differences between groups will become larger with age in the absence of any differential treatment effects (Campbell and Erlebacher, 1970). If this assumption is correct, we would expect middle-class children starting out with a higher level of reading readiness to experience larger gains in test scores over a given period than lower-class children if the two groups are given no special treatment or benefit equally from provided treatment. Thus, any real beneficial effects of treatment given to the lower-income children may be underestimated.

In summary, there is no generally accepted solution to the problem of analyzing data from studies with nonequivalent groups. In fact, some have argued that such comparisons simply should not be made (Cronbach and Furby, 1970; Lord, 1967). However, because the need to assess treatment effects means that such comparisons are made in practical contexts quite frequently, a number of procedures have been developed to try to standardize test scores for the different groups and to correct them for unreliability and for changes in variability over time. For a discussion of some of these techniques and the assumptions they involve, see Cronbach and Furby (1970), Campbell and Boruch (1975), and Magidson (1977).

Interpreting Group by Task Interactions

Issues concerning the response scale

A principle generally taught in experimental design courses is that a researcher must have interval data (data for which the response scale contains equal-sized units between successive scale values) in order to give a valid interpretation of a significant test for interaction. If the sizes of successive units are not equal all along the scale, an interaction in the data is uninterpretable. For analogous reasons, theoretical interpretation of statistical interactions is stymied when the scale used to measure overt performance (say, number of items recalled) is not a linear function of the underlying psychological construct it purports to reflect (memory). Unlike the need for a linear response scale, this problem, which becomes an issue because we want to draw conclusions about theoretical variables rather than just overt performances, is generally ignored. We assume that the external behavior we·measure is a function of the underlying variable of interest, but we do not usually know what kind of relationship exists between the two. If our response measure is a linear function of the underlying construct, then a difference of any particular size at one portion of the response scale will represent the same magnitude of difference, in terms of the underlying variable, as a difference of the same size at any other point along the response sale. If the relationship between the performance measure and the theoretical construct is not linear, this condition will not hold, and the presence or absence of an interaction in a set of data will not have a clear interpretation.

This problem may be illustrated by a simple Group × Task design aimed at assessing the "creativity" of mildly retarded

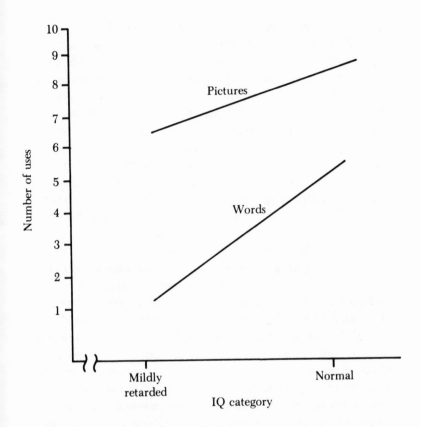

Figure A.1. Hypothetical relationship between IQ, presentation medium, and creativity test score.

and normal-IQ children by scoring each child on the number of different uses she can think of for common objects, which are presented either verbally or as pictures. A graph of some hypothetical data from such an experiment is displayed in figure A.1. Many researchers would be well satisfied to obtain this kind of interaction in the data. (But see the cautionary notes in the discussion of Group × Task designs in chapter 4.) The difference in performance between normal and retarded subjects is greater when items are presented as words than when they are presented as pictures. A naive researcher might want to draw conclusions from such data in terms of a specific deficit involving the verbal associative network of retarded children. However, because pictorial presentation has a generally facilitative effect on performance, scores are higher for both subject groups in the pictures condition than in the words condition. If the relationship between creativity and the number of uses a subject suggests is not a linear one, measured units of difference at the higher end of the scale might in fact represent larger real differences than measured units at the lower end of the scale. (In other words, it might require more creativity to think of an additional use for an item after thinking of seven previous uses than it would after thinking of two previous uses.) It may be that in terms of the underlying dimension of creativity the difference between normals and retarded children is just as great with the pictorial presentation as it is with verbal presentation, or perhaps even greater. Thus, when we want to interpret an interaction in terms of some theoretical construct (and in cognitive psychology we almost always do), we must consider the nature of the relationship between our response scale and whatever it is we are trying to measure. If we do not have a firm basis for assuming that this relationship is a linear one, tests for interactions cannot always be interpreted in a straightforward manner.[3]

A related problem appears when a Group × Task design involves two tests or tasks that use different response scales for measuring the construct of interest. For instance, the difference in memory performance between schizophrenics and normal subjects given a recognition task has been compared to the difference found on a recall task. The nature of the relationship between the two response scales (number of words recalled and number of words recognized) and the underlying construct (memory) is again a critical issue. If a difference of eight words between schizophrenics and normals on a recognition test does not reflect the same size of difference in memory as a difference of eight words on a recall test, the interpretation of interactions in this type of study is problematic.

Task differences in difficulty and reliability

Spurious interaction effects related to a difference in the sensitivity of two tasks to differences in proficiency is another potential problem for a Group × Task design. In psychometric terms, the sensitivity issue is represented by the familiar concept of power of discrimination, the extent to which a test is able to discriminate between good and poor performers. The degree to which a test discriminates among learners of different proficiency levels (within a given group) is related to such features as the average item difficulty, the variability of item difficulties, and the number of items on the test. Chapman and Chapman (1973) have called attention to the impact that differences between experimental tasks in terms of these characteristics (which normally receive little attention when our "tasks" are not standardized tests) can have on whether or not a Group × Task interaction is obtained: "If deficient subjects are as inferior to normal subjects on one ability as on another, but the test that is used to measure one of the abilities is more discriminating than the test of the other, a greater performance deficit will be found on the more discriminating measure" (p. 380).

Because a test's discriminating power is related to difficulty level and because both the tasks and the groups in a Group × Task design frequently vary widely in performance level (as in the hypothetical example of the two creativity tests), spurious interactions may be obtained. Chapman and Chapman illustrate this problem as follows. Usually, items near the 50 percent level of difficulty (items that about half the testees answer successfully) are most discriminating. If we have two groups differing in overall cognitive functioning (such as schizophrenics and normals), and two tasks that differ in difficulty (such as recall of sentences and of random word strings), the following artifacts are possible. If item length, pacing, and so on, are chosen so that the two tests are fairly easy, the sentence recall scores will be toward the easy end of the difficulty scale and the random word strings recall scores will be closer to the 50 percent range. Thus, the recall task with random word strings could be expected to be the higher one in discriminating power and, for this reason alone, should produce the greater mean difference between groups that differ in general proficiency (irrespective of the differences between the processes that are hypothesized to be required for the two tasks). If another researcher uses the same research design but uses longer items, faster pacing, or some other procedural modification that makes both tasks considerably more difficult, the opposite interaction may be obtained. The random words recall test may now be at the hard end of the difficulty scale with the sentence recall scores closer to the 50 percent range. In this case, on the average, the sentence recall test will be more discriminating and may show larger group differences. The extreme cases, of course, are the familiar "floor" and "ceiling" effects, the cases in which any actual group differences on one of the tasks cannot be revealed because the performance of both groups is lumped at the lower or upper limit of the response scale. While experimental psychologists are generally quite sensitive to the fact that a Group × Task design is foiled by a ceiling or floor effect, they have been much less sensitive to the more general problem of effects stemming from less drastic differences between the discriminating powers of different tasks.[4]

Another task characteristic related to discriminating power is reliability, or the degree to which the task yields the same result for each subject on repeated testing (in the absence of learning, treatment effects, or any other change in underlying ability). The actual score a subject obtains on a test is merely an estimate of his true score, that is, of the score he would obtain in the ideal situation where there was no measurement error. The reliability of a test represents the extent to which the observed score correlates with this true score. A number of statisticians and researchers have pointed out that even in the absence of differences in test difficulty, differences in test reliability will affect the size of a Group × Task interaction. Chapman and Chapman have demonstrated this fact empirically. Using two (equally difficult) tests, which we will label Test 1 and Test 2, they selected two subtests of equivalent average difficulty from each. In both cases, one subtest was selected to have a high reliability while the other was selected for low reliability. They administered all four subtests to schizophrenics and to normal subjects. Their data (as displayed in table A.1) showed that if a researcher had used one subtest from Test 1 and one from Test 2 and had happened to choose subtests that differed in reliability, he could have obtained a spurious Group × Task interaction, with the difference between schizophrenics and normals appearing larger on the subtest having the greater reliability. (When subtests of equal reliabilities are compared, the group differences are of the same magnitude on both tests.) This demonstration is particularly revealing because Tests 1 and 2 were not tests of different processes or abilities as they would be in a standard study, but were simply two halves of a single verbal-analogies test.

Most cognitive psychologists have given little consideration to the problem of the artifactual effects that are related to these task characteristics as they interact with group differences. One obvious reason is that experimental tasks are constantly being modified and therefore the necessary data on

Table A.1. Performance of schizophrenic and normal subjects on subtests differing in reliability.

Subjects	Test 1		Test 2	
	High-reliability subtest (coefficient alpha = .80)	Low-reliability subtest (coefficient alpha = .47)	High-reliability subtest (coefficient alpha = .80)	Low-reliability subtest (coefficient alpha = .49)
Normals	6.3	6.5	6.4	6.3
Schizophrenics	3.0	4.2	3.0	4.6
Difference	3.3	2.3	3.4	1.7

Source: Adapted from Chapman and Chapman, 1973, p. 383, Table 1. Copyright 1973 by the American Psychological Association; reprinted by permission.

reliability, difficulty, and discriminating power are generally not available in advance of testing. Educational evaluators, psychometricians, and others who deal in group differences on standardized tests have shown more concern for such measurement issues. Several statistical techniques for coping with these problems have been used, but none of them provides a fully acceptable solution (Cronbach and Furby, 1970). Although we cannot offer a resolution for this issue, we have raised it because we feel that if comparative psychologists are going to base their theoretical conclusions on Group × Task interactions, they need to be highly sensitive to all of the factors that could contribute to artifactual outcomes.

References

Abramyan, L. A. 1977. On the role of verbal instructions in the direction of voluntary movements in children. *Quarterly Newsletter of the Institute for Comparative Human Development*, 1:1-4.

Anderson, J. R. 1972. FRAN: A simulation model of free recall. In G. H. Bower, ed., *The psychology of learning and memory*, vol. 5. New York: Academic Press.

Anderson, J. R., and G. H. Bower. 1972. Recognition and retrieval processes in free recall. *Psychological Review*, 79:97-123.

Anderson, N. H. 1976. How functional measurement can yield validated interval scales of mental quantities. *Journal of Applied Psychology*, 61:677-692.

———. 1980. Information integration theory in developmental psychology. In F. Wilkening, J. Becker, and T. Trabasso, eds., *Information integration by children*. Hillsdale, N. J.: Lawrence Erlbaum Associates.

Anderson, N. H., and D. O. Cuneo. 1978. The height + width rule in children's judgments of quantity. *Journal of Experimental Psychology: General*, 107:335-378.

Atkinson, R. C. 1977. Reflections on psychology's past and concerns about its future. *American Psychologist*, 32:205-210.

Bach, M. J., and B. J. Underwood. 1970. Developmental changes in memory attributes. *Journal of Educational Psychology*, 61:292-296.

Baroff, G. S. 1974. *Mental retardation: nature, cause, and management*. Washington, D.C.: Hemisphere.

Battig, W. F. 1975. Within individual differences in "cognitive" processes. In R. L. Solso, ed., *Information processing and cognition*. Hillsdale, N. J.: Lawrence Erlbaum Associates.

Baylor, G. W., and J. Gascon. 1974. An information processing theory of aspects of the development of weight seriation in children. *Cognitive Psychology*, 6:1-40.

Belmont, J. M., and E. C. Butterfield. 1977. The instructional approach to developmental cognitive research. In R. V. Kail and J. W. Hagen, eds., *Perspectives on the development of memory and cognition.* Hillsdale, N. J.: Lawrence Erlbaum Associates.

Bereiter, C., and S. Engelmann. 1966. *Teaching disadvantaged children in the preschool.* Englewood Cliffs, N. J.: Prentice-Hall.

Berlin, B., and P. Kay. 1969. *Basic color terms: their universality and evolution.* Berkeley: University of California Press.

Berry, J. W. 1968. Ecology, perceptual development and the Muller-Lyer illusion. *British Journal of Psychology*, 59:205-210.

————. 1971. Muller-Lyer susceptibility: culture, ecology or race? *International Journal of Psychology*, 6:193-197.

Blank, M. 1975. Eliciting verbalization from young children in experimental tasks: a methodological note. *Child Development*, 46: 254-257.

Blank, M., L. D. Altman, and W. H. Bridger. 1968. Crossmodal transfer of form discrimination in preschool children. *Psychonomic Science*, 10:51-52.

Blank, M., and S. A. Rose. 1975. Some effects of testing methodology on children's cross-modal performance. *Developmental Psychology*, 11:120.

Bogartz, R. S. 1976. On the meaning of statistical interactions. *Journal of Experimental Child Psychology*, 22:178-183.

Boneau, C. A., and J. M. Circa. 1974. An overview of psychology's human resources: characteristics and salaries from the 1972 APA survey. *American Psychologist*, 24:821-840.

Bornstein, M. H. 1973. Color vision and color naming: a psychological hypothesis of cultural difference. *Psychological Bulletin*, 80:257-285.

Bousfield, W. A. 1953. The occurrence of clustering in the recall of randomly arranged associates. *Journal of General Psychology*, 49:229-240.

Bousfield, W. A., and C. R. Puff. 1964. Clustering as a function of response dominance. *Journal of Experimental Psychology*, 67:76-79.

Brown, A. L. 1972. A rehearsal deficit in retardates' continuous short term memory: keeping track of variables that have few or many states. *Psychonomic Science*, 29:373-376.

———. 1978. Knowing when, where, and how to remember: a problem of metacognition. In R. Glaser, ed., *Advances in instructional psychology*, vol. 1. Hillsdale, N. J.: Lawrence Erlbaum Associates.

Brown, A. L., and C. R. Barclay. 1976. The effects of training specific mnemonics on the metamnemonic efficiency of retarded children. *Child Development*, 47:71-80.

Brown, A. L., and J. C. Campione. 1977. Memory strategies in learning: training children to study strategically. In H. Pick, H. Leibowitz, J. Singer, A. Steinschneider, and H. Stevenson, eds., *Applications of basic research in psychology*. New York: Plenum Press.

Brown, A. L., and J. C. Campione. 1978. Permissible inferences from the outcome of training studies in cognitive development research. *Newsletter of the Institute of Comparative Human Development*, 2:46-53.

Brown, A. L., J. C. Campione, N. W. Bray, and B. L. Wilcox. 1973. Keeping track of changing variables: effects of rehearsal training and rehearsal prevention in normal and retarded adolescents. *Journal of Experimental Psychology*, 101:123-131.

Brown, A. L., J. C. Campione, and M. D. Murphy. 1974. Keeping track of changing variables: long-term retention of a trained rehearsal strategy by retarded adolescents. *American Journal of Mental Deficiency*, 78:446-453.

Brown, A. L., and J. S. DeLoache. 1978. Skills, plans, and self-regulation. In R. Siegler, ed., *Children's thinking: what develops?* Hillsdale, N. J.: Lawrence Erlbaum Associates.

Brown, R. 1964. Discussion of the conference. *Transcultural studies in cognition*. Special publication of *American Anthropologist*, 66:243-253, eds. A. K. Romney and R. G. D'Andrade. Menasha, Wis.: American Anthropological Association.

Brown, R., and E. Lenneberg. 1954. A study in language and cognition. *Journal of Abnormal and Social Psychology*, 49:454-462.

Bryant, P. 1974. *Perception and understanding in young children*. New York: Basic Books.

Butterfield, E. C., and J. M. Belmont. 1977. Assessing and improving the executive cognitive functions of mentally retarded people. In I. Bialer and M. Sternlicht, eds., *Psychological issues in mental retardation*. New York: Psychological Dimensions.

Butterfield, E. C., C. Wambold, and J. M. Belmont. 1973. On the theory and practice of improving short-term memory. *American Journal of Mental Deficiency*, 77:654-669.

Campbell, D. T., and R. F. Boruch. 1975. Making the case for randomized assignment to treatments by considering the alternatives: six ways in which quasi-experimental evaluations in compensatory education tend to underestimate effects. In C. A. Bennett and A. A. Lumsdaine, eds., *Evaluation and experiment: some critical issues in assessing social programs*. New York: Academic Press.

Campbell, D. T., and A. E. Erlebacher. 1970. How regression artifacts in quasi-experimental evaluations can mistakenly make compensatory education look harmful. In J. Hellmuth, ed., *Compensatory education: a national debate* (vol. 3, *Disadvantaged child*). New York: Brunner/Mazel.

Campbell, D. T., and J. C. Stanley. 1963. *Experimental and quasi-experimental designs for research*. Chicago: Rand McNally.

Chapman, L. J., and J. P. Chapman. 1973. Problems in the measurement of cognitive deficit. *Psychological Bulletin*, 79:380-385.

Chi, M. T. H. 1978. Knowledge structures and memory development. In R. S. Siegler, ed., *Children's thinking: what develops?* Hillsdale, N. J.: Lawrence Erlbaum Associates.

Cofer, C. N. 1965. On some factors in the organizational characteristics of free recall. *American Psychologist*, 20:261-272.

Cofer, C. N. 1966. Some evidence for coding processes derived from clustering in free recall. *Journal of Verbal Learning and Verbal Behavior*, 5:188-192.

Cofer, C. N., D. R. Bruce, and G. M. Reicher. 1966. Clustering in free recall as a function of certain methodogical variations. *Journal of Experimental Psychology*, 71:858-866.

Cole, M. 1976. A probe trial procedure for the study of children's discrimination learning and transfer. *Journal of Experimental Child Psychology*, 22:499-510.

Cole, M., J. Gay, and J. Glick. 1968. A cross-cultural investigation of information processing. *International Journal of Psychology*, 3:93-102.

Cole, M., L. Hood, and R. McDermott. 1978. Ecological niche picking: ecological invalidity as an axiom of experimental, cognitive psychology. Working paper, Rockefeller University, New York.

Cook, T. D., and D. T. Campbell. 1976. The design and conduct of quasi-experiments and true experiments in field settings. In M. D. Dunnette, ed., *Handbook of industrial and organizational psychology.* Chicago: Rand McNally.

Covington, M. V., R. S. Crutchfield, L. B. Davies, and R. M. Olton. 1974. *The productive thinking program: a course in learning to think.* Columbus, Ohio: Merrill.

Cramer, P. 1973. Evidence for a developmental shift in the basis of memory organization. *Journal of Experimental Child Psychology,* 16:12-22.

Cronbach, L. J., and L. Furby. 1970. How should we measure "change" — or should we? *Psychological Bulletin,* 74:68-80.

Deregowski, J. B. 1972. Reproduction of orientation of Kohs-type figures: a cross-cultural study. *British Journal of Psychology,* 63:283-296.

Deutsch, M. R. 1967. *The disadvantaged child: selected papers of Martin Deutsch and associates.* New York: Basic Books.

Edgerton, R. B. 1967. *The cloak of competence.* Berkeley: University of California Press.

Executive Office of the President, Office of Management and Budget. *Special analyses, budget of the U.S. Government, fiscal year, 1978.* Washington, D.C.: U.S. Government Printing Office, 1977.

Farnham-Diggory, S. 1972. *Cognitive processes in education.* New York: Harper and Row.

Felzen, D., and M. Anisfeld. 1970. Semantic and phonetic relations in the false recognition of words by third- and sixth-grade children. *Developmental Psychology,* 3:163-168.

Freund, J. S., and J. W. Johnson. 1972. Changes in memory attribute dominance as a function of age. *Journal of Educational Psychology,* 63:386-389.

Frost, J. L., and G. T. Rowland. 1971. *Compensatory programming: the acid test of American education.* Dubuque: W. C. Brown.

Goodnow, J. 1976. The nature of intelligent behavior: questions raised by cross-cultural research. In L. B. Resnick, ed., *The nature of intelligence.* Hillsdale, N. J.: Lawrence Erlbaum Associates.

Hale, G. A., and J. Flaugher. 1977. Distraction effects in tasks of varying difficulty: methodological issues in measuring development of distractibility. *Journal of Experimental Child Psychology,* 24: 212-218.

Hale, G. A., and J. Flaugher. 1977. Distraction effects in tasks of varying difficulty: methodological issues in measuring development of distractibility. *Journal of Experimental Child Psychology*, 24: 212-218.

Hale, G. A., and E. E. Stevenson, Jr. 1974. The effects of auditory and visual distractors on children's performance in a short-term memory task. *Journal of Experimental Child Psychology*, 18: 280-292.

Hall, J. W., and M. S. Halperin. 1972. The development of memory encoding processes in young children. *Developmental Psychology*, 6:181.

Hall, V. C., R. Salvi, L. Seggev, and E. Caldwell. 1970. Cognitive synthesis, conservation and task analysis. *Developmental Psychology*, 2:423-428.

Heider, E. R. 1972. Universals in color naming and memory. *Journal of Experimental Psychology*, 93:10-20.

Istomina, Z. M. 1975. The development of voluntary memory in preschool-age children. *Soviet Psychology*, 13:5-64.

Jahoda, G. 1966. Geometric illusions and environment: a study in Ghana. *British Journal of Psychology*, 57:193-199.

———. 1971. Retinal pigmentation, illusion susceptibility and space perception. *International Journal of Psychology*, 6:99-208.

———. 1975. Retinal pigmentation and space perception: a failure to replicate. *Journal of Social Psychology*, 97:133-134.

Jenkins, J. J., W. D. Mink, and W. A. Russell. 1958. Associative clustering as a function of verbal associative strength. *Psychological Reports*, 4:127-136.

Jenkins, J. J., and W. A. Russell. 1952. Associative clustering during recall. *Journal of Abnormal and Social Psychology*, 47:818-821.

Keeney, T. J., S. R. Cannizzo, and J. H. Flavell. 1967. Spontaneous and induced verbal rehearsal in a recall task. *Child Development*, 38:953-966.

Kellas, G., C. McCauley, and C. F. McFarland. 1975. Developmental aspects of storage and retrieval. *Journal of Experimental Child Psychology*, 19:51-62.

Kendler, H. H., and T. S. Kendler. 1962. Vertical and horizontal processes in problem solving. *Psychological Review*, 69:1-16.

Klahr, D. 1976. Steps toward the simulation of intellectual development. In L. B. Resnick, ed., *The nature of intelligence*. Hillsdale, N. J.: Lawrence Erlbaum Associates.

Klahr, D., and J. G. Wallace. 1970. An information processing analysis of some Piagetian experimental tasks. *Cognitive Psychology*, 1:350-387.

Klahr, D., and J. G. Wallace. 1976. *Cognitive development: an information processing view*. Hillsdale, N. J.: Lawrence Erlbaum Associates.

Krantz, D. H., and A. Tversky. 1971. Conjoint-measurement analysis of composition rules in psychology. *Psychological Review*, 78: 151-169.

Kreutzer, M. S., C. Leonard, and J. H. Flavell. 1975. An interview of children's knowledge about memory. *Monographs of the Society for Research in Child Development*, 40 (1, serial no. 159).

Labov, W. 1970. *The study of nonstandard English*. Champaign, Ill.: National Council of Teachers of English.

Levine, M. 1966. Hypothesis behavior by humans during discrimination learning. *Journal of Experimental Psychology*, 71:331-338.

Loftus, G. R. 1978. On interpretation of interactions. *Memory and Cognition*, 6:312-319.

Lord, F. M. 1967. A paradox of the interpretation of group comparisons. *Psychological Bulletin*, 68:304-305.

Lucy, J. A., and R. A. Shweder. 1979. Whorf and his critics: linguistic and nonlinguistic influences on color memory. *American Anthropologist*, 81:581-615.

Magidson, J. 1977. Toward a causal model approach for adjusting for preexisting differences in the nonequivalent control group situation: a general alternative to ANCOVA. *Evaluation Quarterly*, 1:399-420.

Mandler, G. 1967. Organization and memory. In K. W. Spence and J. T. Spence, eds., *The psychology of learning and motivation*, vol. 1. New York: Academic Press.

Mandler, G., and Z. Pearlstone. 1966. Free and constrained concept learning and subsequent recall. *Journal of Verbal Learning and Verbal Behavior*, 5:126-131.

Marshall, G. R. 1967. Stimulus characteristics contributing to organization in free recall. *Journal of Verbal Learning and Verbal Behavior*, 6:364-374.

McGarrigle, J., and M. Donaldson. 1974-75. Conservation accidents. *Cognition*, 3:341-350.

Means, B., and W. D. Rohwer, Jr. 1976. Attribute dominance in memory development. *Developmental Psychology*, 12:411-417.

Medin, D. L. 1975. A theory of context in discrimination learning. In G. H. Bower, ed., *The psychology of learning and motivation*, vol. 9. New York: Academic Press.

Medin, D. L., and M. Cole. 1975. Comparative psychology and human cognition. In W. K. Estes, ed., *Handbook of learning and cognitive processes*. Hillsdale, N. J.: Lawrence Erlbaum Associates.

Mehren, W. A., and I. J. Lehmann. 1980. *Standarized tests in education*. New York: Holt, Rinehart, and Winston.

Mistler-Lachman, J. L. 1977. Spontaneous shift in encoding dimensions among elderly subjects. *Journal of Gerontology*, 32:68-72.

Neisser, U., and J. Hupcey. 1974. A Sherlockian experiment. *Cognition*, 3:307-311.

Newell, A., and H. A. Simon. 1972. *Human problem solving*. Englewood Cliffs, N. J.: Prentice-Hall.

Nisbett, R. E., and T. D. Wilson. 1977. Telling more than we can know: verbal reports on mental processes. *Psychological Review*, 84:231-259.

Norman, D. A., and D. G. Bobrow. 1975. On data-limited and resource-limited processes. *Cognitive Psychology*, 7:44-64.

Olton, R. M., and R. S. Crutchfield. 1969. Developing the skills of productive thinking. In P. Mussen, J. Langer, and M. Covington, eds., *Trends and issues in developmental psychology*. New York: Holt, Rinehart, and Winston.

Pollack, R. H. 1970. Muller-Lyer illusion: effect of age, lightness contrast and hue. *Science*, 170:93-94.

Pollack, R. H., and S. D. Silvar. 1967. Magnitude of the Muller-Lyer illusion in children as a function of the pigmentations of the fundus oculi. *Psychonomic Science*, 8:83-84.

Resnick, L. B., and R. Glaser. 1976. Problem solving and intelligence. In L. B. Resnick, ed., *The nature of intelligence*. Hillsdale, N. J.: Lawrence Erlbaum Associates.

Richard, J. F., E. Cauzinelle, and J. Mathieu. 1973. Logical and memory processes in a unidimensional concept identification task by children and adults. *Acta Psychologica*, 37:315-331.

Richman, C. L., S. Nida, and L. Pittman. 1976. Effects of meaningfulness on child free-recall learning. *Developmental Psychology*, 12:460-465.

Rivers, W. H. R. 1901. Introduction and vision. In A. C. Hadden, ed.,

Reports of the Cambridge anthropological expeditions to the Torres Straits. Cambridge, England: University Press.

———. 1905. Observations on the sense of the Todas. *British Journal of Psychology*, 1:321-396.

Rohwer, W. D., Jr. 1973. Elaboration and learning in childhood and adolescence. In H. W. Reese, ed., *Advances in child development and behavior*, vol. 8. New York: Academic Press.

———. 1976. An introduction to research on individual and developmental differences in learning. In W. K. Estes, ed., *Handbook of learning and cognitive processes*, vol. 3. Hillsdale, N. J.: Lawrence Erlbaum Associates.

Rosch, E. 1977. Human categorization. In N. Warren, ed., *Studies in cross-cultural psychology*. New York: Academic Press.

Rose, S. A., and M. Blank. 1974. The potency of context in children's cognition: an illustration through conservation. *Child Development*, 45:499-502.

Schneider, S. F. 1979. Positions of psychologists trained for research. Unpublished manuscript. Washington, D.C.: National Institute of Mental Health.

Scribner, S., and M. Cole. 1972. Effects of constrained recall training on children's performance in a verbal memory task. *Child Development*, 43:845-857.

Segall, M. H., D. T. Campbell, and M. J. Herskovits. 1966. *The influence of culture on visual perception.* New York: Bobbs-Merrill.

Serpell, R. 1971a. Discrimination of orientation by Zambian children. *Journal of Comparative and Physiological Psychology*, 75:312-316.

———. 1971b. Preference for specific orientation of abstract shapes among Zambian children. *Journal of Cross-Cultural Psychology*, 2:225-239.

Serpell, R., and J. B. Deregowski. 1972. Teaching pictorial depth perception: a classroom study. *Human Development Research Reports*, no. 21. Lusaka: University of Zambia.

Shatz, M. 1977. The relationship between cognitive processes and the development of communication skills. In B. Keasey, ed., *Nebraska symposium on motivation*. Lincoln: University of Nebraska Press.

Siegler, R. S. 1975. Defining the locus of developmental differences in children's causal reasoning. *Journal of Experimental Child Psychology*, 20:512-525.

———. 1976. Three aspects of cognitive development. *Cognitive Psychology*, 8:481-520.

———. 1978. The origins of scientific reasoning. In R. S. Siegler, ed., *Children's thinking: what develops?* Hillsdale, N. J.: Lawrence Erlbaum Associates.

Siegler, R. S., and S. Vago. 1978. The development of a proportionality concept: judging relative fullness. *Journal of Experimental Child Psychology*, 25:371-395.

Sigel, I. E. 1970. The distancing hypothesis: a causal hypothesis for the acquisition of representational thought. In M. R. Jones, ed., *Miami symposium on the prediction of behavior, 1968: effects of early experience.* Coral Gables: University of Miami Press.

Sigel, I. E., L. M. Anderson, and H. Shapiro. 1966. Categorization behavior of lower- and middle-class Negro preschool children: differences in dealing with representation of familiar objects. *Journal of Negro Education*, 35:218-229.

Sigel, I. E., and B. McBane. 1967. Cognitive competence and level of symbolization among five-year-old children. In J. Hellmuth, ed., *The disadvantaged child*, vol. 1. New York: Brunner/Mazel.

Sigel, I. E., and Olmsted, P. P. 1970. Modification of classificatory competence and level of representation among lower-class Negro kindergarten children. In H. Passow, ed., *Education in depressed groups*, vol. 2. New York: Columbia University Teachers College Press.

Simmons, W. 1979. The effects of the cultural salience of test materials on social class and ethnic differences in cognitive performance. *The Quarterly Newsletter of the Laboratory of Comparative Human Cognition*, 1:43-47.

Singleton, W. T. 1977. *The analysis of practical skills.* London: MTP Press.

Stolz, W. S., and J. Tiffany. 1972. The production of "child-like" word associations by adults to unfamiliar adjectives. *Journal of Verbal Learning and Verbal Behavior*, 11:38-46.

Taylor, I. W., and W. W. Taylor. 1962. Provisions for the educable mentally retarded in the United States. In F. J. Schonell, J. McLeod, and R. G. Cochrane, eds., *The slow learner.* St. Lucia: University of Queensland Press.

Tighe, T. J., and L. S. Tighe. 1972. Stimulus control in children's discrimination learning. In A. D. Pick, ed., *Minnesota symposia on child psychology*, vol. 6. Minneapolis: University of Minnesota Press.

Underwood, B. J. 1957. *Psychological research*. New York: Appleton-Century-Crofts.

―――. 1969. Attributes of memory. *Psychological Review*, 76:559-573.

Vygotsky, L. S. 1978. *Mind in society*, eds. M. Cole, V. John-Steiner, S. Scribner, and E. Souberman. Cambridge: Harvard University Press.

Whorf, B. L. 1956. *Language, thought, and reality*. Cambridge: MIT Press.

Wood, G. 1974. Fundamentals of psychological research. Boston: Little, Brown.

Wood, G., and B. J. Underwood. 1967. Implicit responses and conceptual similarity. *Journal of Verbal Learning and Verbal Behavior*, 6:1-10.

Zigler, E. 1966. Motivational determinants in the performance of retarded children. *American Journal of Orthopsychiatry*, 36:848-856.

Notes

2. The Normative Logic of Experimental Design

1. We have laid out the components of a research program as a series of sequential steps in order to make their respective characteristics clearer. In practice, however, these components are not necessarily pursued separately or in the order listed.

2. This requirement for an objective description of the phenomenon under study calls for a narrow, operational definition of the variable to be investigated. A researcher interested in achievement motivation, for example, might operationalize that concept as achievement need score on the Thematic Apperception Test (TAT). However, it is still the general concept of achievement motivation that the researcher is interested in rather than the score on the TAT achievement scale per se. When the true target of interest is more general than the operationally defined phenomenon, multiple measures (in effect, multiple operational definitions) need to be examined. Many of the most fallacious statements in the comparative literature concern what different groups supposedly *cannot* do. Such statements reflect a tendency to draw conclusions about general, theoretical constructs on the basis of research with a single, narrowly defined measure of that construct.

3. Random assignment produces groups that will be equivalent in terms of all these characteristics *in the long run*, that is, with very large numbers of subjects. With the relatively small numbers of subjects used in laboratory experiments, treatment groups are usually not equivalent in terms of all individual differences. However, inferential statistics takes this factor into account, and as long as subject assignment is random, the rules of hypothesis testing minimize the probability that an experimenter will accept as significant a performance difference be-

tween treatment groups resulting from preexperimental differences in the subjects assigned to the two conditions.

4. In practice, however, the ability of any piece of research to rule out a hypothesis is open to challenge. If it is not universally agreed that the process theory would have to lead to the specified prediction under the conditions of the experiment, failure to confirm the prediction is not critical for the hypothesis.

5. To simplify our discussion, we have described the list-tagging process as if it were always successful. In the actual model, tagging is a probabilistic process in which FRAN's attempts at tagging nodes and pathways fail with a specified probability.

3. What Happens When All Other Things Are Not Equal?

1. Sometimes the researcher, instead of directly comparing different groups, may be trying out the methods and materials developed with one group on another special group (e.g., administering a set of Piagetian tasks to retarded children). In such cases the express interest may be in studying the functioning of the special group in its own right without necessarily drawing comparisons with the standard group. If one's purpose is really limited in this way, group differences are not measured and thus the theoretical problems involved in trying to attribute them to any one subject variable do not arise. However, there is always a strong temptation to contrast the findings of research with the special group with the results of other research with some other subject population. Some of the most questionable generalizations in the comparative literature have stemmed from such post hoc comparisons of special and standard groups tested in different studies, by different experimenters, under different conditions.

Whether one is interested in drawing comparative conclusions or just in studying the special group in its own right, the problems we will raise concerning equivalence of treatment are relevant. If the instructions, materials, and procedures borrowed from noncomparative cognitive psychology do not mean the same thing for members of the special group as for members of the group with which they were developed, we are no longer testing what we thought we were. Consequently, results from such studies are often puzzling or extremely misleading, even if no cross-group comparisons are to be made.

2. In practice, such matching would be very difficult to achieve.

3. In reference to obtained developmental differences in susceptibility to the illusion, it is interesting to note that density of eye pigmentation also increases with age.

4. Another apt demonstration of this sort of effect has been made by Hall, Salvi, Seggev, and Caldwell (1970) using a pseudoreading task that had been interpreted by some researchers as showing preschoolers' lack of "neurological readiness" for the kind of "cognitive synthesis" required in reading.

5. A difference in recall levels between blocked and randomly ordered list groups would corroborate the interpretation that blocking was having an effect on list organization, but there was no difference in recall levels for the two presentation formats in the study on which our illustration is based.

4. Comparing Tasks and Groups

1. The same problem exists when experimenters try to make quantitative comparisons across distractor types.

2. Subsequently this work was called into question by Lucy and Shweder (1978) on the grounds that Rosch's evidence concerning codability was inadequate to her strong conclusion that focality, not codability, controlled remembering. Their criticisms are based upon a careful analysis of the stimulus arrays and the subtasks that make up the overall experiment contrived by Rosch. That Rosch could correctly predict a pattern of responding within cultures that could be matched across cultures, yet err in her attribution of cause to factors within the experiment, strongly reinforces our contention that *both* a strong theory of the kind of thinking demanded by cognitive tasks and a careful arrangement of comparisons to rule out confounding artifacts must be part of the overall comparative cognitive enterprise.

Readers interested in this research topic might refer to Bornstein (1973), who hypothesizes that variations among cultures' color-naming systems are a by-product of physiological differences. Bornstein suggests that the increased exposure to ultraviolet radiation associated with living at high altitudes or near the equator results in denser eye pigmentation, which in turn causes reduced sensitivity to the short-wavelength end of the color spectrum. Because blue and green are difficult for people with densely pigmented eyes to discriminate, Bornstein suggests that it is perfectly reasonable that their color-naming systems should use one word to refer to both blue and green (and, in extreme cases, to black as well). Hence, an area of research originally stimulated by the notion that differences in language result in differences in perception has now produced the opposite hypothesis — that physiologically based differences in perception are responsible for differences in color language.

3. Another form of the Group × Task research strategy entails devising a modified task in which the process hypothesized to produce one group's superiority on the standard task should result in *poorer* performance rather than facilitation. For example, if older children are presumed to have better memory for picture paired associates than their younger counterparts because they verbally label the pictures, the researcher might design a variation of the recall task in which verbal labeling should impede performance. For instance, the modified task might employ paired associates in which the response items in some pairs are pictures whose names are homophones for the response items in other pairs (for example, cow-flour and train-flower). If the usual ordering of group proficiencies is reversed on the modified task (that is, if younger children perform better than older children on the homophone version of the paired-associate task), the researcher has some support for his hypothesis relating group differences on the standard task to the process variable presumably being manipulated (verbalization). Such a disordinal interaction in the data is particularly impressive since most potential artifactual sources for group differences would favor the older group. However, the caveats concerning the dependence of the Group × Task research strategy on careful task analyses and the selection of comparable tasks are equally relevant to this variant of the strategy. Moreover, interpreting the outcome of this type of research is difficult when the hoped-for outcome is not attained — when the normally proficient subjects do not perform more poorly than the normally improficient on the modified version of the task. In such cases, it is unclear whether the failure to obtain the predicted outcome stems from a faulty hypothesis about the role the process plays in task performance or from the canceling out of the negative impact of using the process in the modified task by the positive impact of other variables in terms of which the normally proficient subjects are at an advantage (such as attention, familiarity with

the stimuli, or elaboration strategies). We have chosen to illustrate the Group × Task approach with the ordinal interaction (where two groups perform equivalently on one task but differ in proficiency on the other) rather than this disordinal interaction version of the strategy because the former is more commonly used and is more consonant with applied concerns, which focus on improving the performance of the deficient rather than impairing that of the proficient.

4. The interpretation of Group × Task interactions is complicated further by certain statistical issues that become particularly troublesome when groups differ in performance on the control (or compensatory) task as well as on the experimental task. Some of these issues are treated in the appendix.

5. It is still a question how much improvement we must see in order to conclude that lack of rehearsal was indeed the source of the younger child's difficulties. Researchers differ in the standards they adopt. The weakest standard, and hence the most likely to yield "success," is that of statistically significant improvement. Belmont and Butterfield (1977), who have done much to explicate the logic of the training approach, suggest that the performance level of an adult sample without special training is a reasonable standard for establishing the success of training effects. Rohwer's criterion would be the performance level of an older sample receiving the same compensatory condition as the less proficient group.

5. Model-based Approaches

1. Other models (for instance, responsibility judgments based on intent alone) may also be plausible and can be similarly tested through the functional measurement technique.

2. The use of this model is surprising both because it is inconsistent with the interpretation that the five-year-old centrates on a single dimension and because it is quite counterintuitive. Even the most global, nonanalytic perception of area would seemingly be a multiplicative function of height and width (Anderson and Cuneo, 1978).

3. In a more recent study, Hale and Flaugher (1977) addressed this issue. They found that if the effect of distraction is measured in absolute terms, there are no age differences in distractibility, but if it is measured in proportional terms, there are.

6. From Laboratory to Life

1. We are *not* arguing that comparative research is not worth-while unless these assumptions are met. On the contrary, we believe that basic research aimed at developing an understanding of fundamental cognitive processes must be the cornerstone for theories of comparative psychology and that in the long run such research will provide the firmest foundation for efforts to improve cognitive functioning. It is not cognitive research itself but its immediate application to practical problems that is dependent upon these assumptions.

2. A series of interviews conducted by Edgerton (1967) with retarded individuals some years after their release from a state institution suggests that mildly retarded individuals themselves disagree with Baroff's conclusion. In the words of one mildly retarded man: "Most of us people that was at the colony [the institution for the retarded] just can't figure [do arithmetic] . . . Outside you gotta learn to figure or you'll go down the old pot. Seems like most of us go down the pot" (p. 217).

Appendix. Statistical Issues in Comparative Research

1. In his discussion of the best way to resolve this problem, Underwood appears to use the same tactic of relating group differences to process differences that underlies the various comparative research strategies we have described: "As I view this situation escape comes only by the use of some form of theoretical approach . . . in investigations in which subject variables have been attacked with some degree of success, certain working hypotheses have been first advanced and the implications of these hypotheses explored by research. More specifically, these working hypotheses *relate the subject variables to fundamental behavioral processes* . . . The investigator starts out with an idea or hypothesis that differences in subject variables (such as differences in severity of schizophrenia) reflect the operation of more fundamental processes. What he says, in effect, is if this difference is due to this or that process . . . then he would expect this (difference in rigidity) to obtain. He is applying a set of principles of behavior about which we already know considerable to another area of behavior other than that used to derive the principles in the first place. If a reasonable number of tests of the implications of the application are positive we then begin to accept the original hypothesis which identified differences in a sub-

ject variable with a difference in a more fundamental process" (pp. 117-118).

2. Statistical regression effects are not limited to cases where the matching is done on the basis of a pretest of the variable used as the outcome measure. The same problem occurs when matching is done on any variable related to the dependent variable. The matching procedure used in the first of Berry's studies of Muller-Lyer illusion susceptibility described in chapter 3 can be used as an example. Berry matched his comparison groups in terms of scores on the Koh's blocks test of perceptual development. Because the total urban Eskimo sample scored higher than the total rural-traditional Eskimo sample, matching required selecting a subgroup of low-scoring urban Eskimos to compare with a subgroup of high-scoring rural Eskimos. If greater perceptual development is linked to a drop in illusion susceptibility as hypothesized, a finding of greater susceptibility among the rural group (or a failure to find a difference between the groups) could have been attributed to statistical regression. (Since Berry found greater susceptibility among the urban group, his results were not clouded by this problem of interpretation.)

3. Some outcomes will be interpretable without the assumption of a linear relationship between the response measure and the theoretical construct. As Loftus (1978) has indicated, in the most common case, where all we can reasonably assume is that the response is monotonically related to the underlying variable (that is, for any increase in the underlying variable there is an increase of some size in the response measure), an obtained interaction is interpretable if it is a disordinal (crossover) one, and the absence of an interaction is interpretable if one or both of the main effects are not significant. If the nature of the relationship between the response scale and the underlying variable can be more fully specified (for example, as a negatively accelerated function), a somewhat larger number of outcomes becomes interpretable. To pursue the issue further, see Loftus for a description of these interpretable outcomes and Krantz and Tversky (1971) for a method of determining whether an interaction obtained in a complex design could be eliminated if the date were subjected to some nonlinear transformation.

4. This problem does not exist in the case of a disordinal interaction, in which one group scores higher on the first test and the other group excels on the second. In the more frequent case of an ordinal in-

teraction, the researcher can perform a minimal check on her data. If the larger group difference occurs on the task in which overall difficulty is closer to the middle range rather than on that with the more extreme difficulty level, it is unlikely that task differences in discriminating power are responsible for the Group × Task interaction.

Index